**REVELATION
A PROTESTANT VIEW**

REVELATION

A Protestant View.

The Dogmatic Constitution
on
Divine Revelation

A COMMENTARY
by
Roger Schutz and Max Thurian

Preface by
Henri de Lubac, S.J.

NEWMAN PRESS

Westminster, Md.   New York, N.Y.   Glen Rock, N.J.

Amsterdam   Toronto   Montreal

A Newman Press Edition, originally published under the title *La parole vivante au concile* by Les Presses de Taizé, Saône-et-Loire, France, © 1966. Translation by Kathryn Sullivan, R.S.C.J. The text of the Dogmatic Constitution was translated by George H. Tavard, A.A., and appeared together with his commentary in *Dogmatic Constitution on Divine Revelation of Vatican Council II* (Paulist Press, © 1966).

Library of Congress
Catalog Card Number: 68-21453

Published by Newman Press
Editorial Office: 304 W. 58th St., N.Y., N.Y. 10019
Business Office: Westminster, Maryland 21157

Printed and bound in the
United States of America

CONTENTS

CONTENTS

PREFACE

The Spirit breathes where it wills. At the very moment when many among us, as if suddenly struck blind, no longer perceive the beauty nor the value for the world of the words of the Gospel which are the source and norm of the Church's religious life, on the plateau of Taizé, a neighboring dependency of ancient Cluny, a group of young men come from every section of the Protestant Reform to lead in common the life they have rediscovered in all its freshness. Again, at the very moment when many among us, seized by a kind of mental dizziness, seem to be on the verge of weakening in our attachment to the Tradition of the Church which transmits to us the word of God in all its living actuality, it is at this exact moment that from Taizé comes to us a new book that can strengthen our attachment. *Revelation: A Protestant View* is a beautiful testimony of faith.

But above all it is a work of solid information. After a brief preliminary chapter describing a day at the Council for the Brothers of Taizé then present in Rome, there follows a translation of the Dogmatic Constitution *Dei Verbum* on revelation and then a point by point commentary on the text. The two authors, Roger Schutz and Max Thurian, were ideally situated to give us this commentary; they were near enough to follow each phase of the preparation of the Council text, were interested in even the least details of its editing, and for a long time nothing meant more to them than this fundamental subject. Yet precisely because of this interest one might have feared that they would more or less yield—as has happened in other writings on the Council—to the temptation to use the author-

1

ity of text to support some personal ideas of their own. Perhaps
one could fear at least that the ecumenical fervor prevailing at
Taizé would unconsciously influence them to adopt an extreme
interpretation of a text which certainly affords them new support. But this is not the case. Here is a perfectly objective
commentary whose gravity, clarity, and balance make it an ex-
cellent working instrument.

Many details of interpretation, which are far from unim-
portant, are explained, thanks to a thorough understanding
of the debates. This is true of such expressions as, "the Tradition that issues from the apostles," or "the understanding of
spiritual realities that comes from experience," or "salutary
truth" with its doublet, "the truth that God decided to put
down in the sacred writings for our salvation's sake," or again,
"all Church proclamation must feed on, and be ruled by, Holy
Scripture." After a comparative study of several passages and
their various nuances, the assimilation of Scripture to the Word
of God is delicately analyzed. An appraisal of the analogies
and especially of the differences of perspective of the two
Vatican Councils makes possible a just appreciation of today's
doctrinal orientations.

It is only right that the second chapter of the Constitution
on the transmission of divine revelation requires the lengthy
consideration of the commentators as it did of those who composed it. The commentators seek to clarify as far as possible
the idea of Tradition that is here expressed both in relation
to revelation itself and in relation to Holy Scripture. It is also
in connection with this chapter (completed by some statements
drawn from the sixth chapter) that they confront Catholic
doctrine.

There again they proceed with the greatest of clarity. Guided
by definitions given in Montreal in 1963 by the Fourth World
Conference on Faith and Order, they begin by distinguishing
four different uses of the word "tradition" not so much to
criticize the Council but to establish that the word cannot be
understood univocally in its different contexts. Rightly do they

insist that this creates a difficulty for the exegesis of the Constitution. This does not prevent them from going on to show
their substantial agreement about the triple role accorded
Tradition in the formation of Scripture, then in its interpretation and lastly in making its message relevant for every Christian generation—an agreement easily reached because the
Council explicitly attributes the efficacy of this triple role to
the action of the Holy Spirit.

Between those Catholics who have most willingly followed
the path traced by the Council and the Protestants who are
the most sympathetic, there are, however, certain shades of
difference in the way of explaining or in actually using Holy
Scripture in the life of the Church. It is hard to find even a
trace of these slight differences in the present commentary. In
our opinion the only serious point of friction to be found in
this area between Catholics and Protestants, the only question
whose answer still seriously separates Christians, is that of
knowing what ought to be the final criterion of the interpretation of Scripture, or, in other words, how authentic Tradition
can be identified.

We place this final criterion in the authority of the magis-
terium of the Church. Protestantism thinks this is dangerous.
It fears that such a magisterium "ultimately places itself above
Scripture and cannot itself be judged by the Word of God."
To which we continue to answer with St. Francis of Sales, that
according to our way of thinking it is not Scripture that needs
an outside rule or light, but our glosses; we do not place a
judge between God and ourselves but "between a man like
Calvin and another man like Morus" (cf. Lajeunie, *Saint
François de Sales et l'esprit salésien*).

Roger Schutz and Max Thurian observe that on this point
the conciliar text does not give "an answer that Protestantism
can accept as sufficient." Yet they are not unaware that "an
important advance has been made" on the road to an agreement. They see "an ecumenical sign" in the fact that this text
at least affirms unambiguously that the magisterium can never

propose to our faith anything other than the content of the Word of God and that the authority in the Church is not "above" this Word, but entirely at its service. Their moderation and their sympathy are not tendentious. They are perspicacious. Consequently they are able to pronounce in depth on the general character of the whole Constitution.

It is known that the Council Fathers wished to avoid a solution of the now famous disagreement known as "the two sources" so that theological schools could freely discuss a topic which is of capital interest to our separated brothers. But if they did not settle the quarrel, it is not that they left things just as they were. The Constitution brings "new light" which profoundly modifies the terms and therefore should considerably lessen the differences. Neither Scripture nor Tradition can hereafter appear as "sources." On the other hand, the concrete and unified idea of revelation proposed in the first chapter prevents the least material division of its content into separate channels.

Consequently, neither Tradition, nor Scripture, appear diminished; what is granted to one is not taken from the other. Quite the contrary. And there is good reason to hope that without having placed any group in the Church in the wrong, the promulgation of *Dei Verbum* will have this happy result, among others, of reducing reasons for disagreement among Catholic theologians and at the same time of preparing the basis for a more complete understanding among Christian confessions.

But if our authors give special attention to this crucial problem, they do not stop there. What gives great interest to their commentary is that apart from the problem we have just taken as an example, they generalize their observations. Not only in the Constitution on Divine Revelation but in the whole work of the Council, they think they can detect the operation of a "method" or an "attempt" or an "ecumenical and inclusive advance" which transcends and subsumes a whole series of unfavorable positions, believed at first to be mutually exclusive.

Casting a glance over the doctrinal history of recent centuries, they point out that Catholic theologians, reacting against certain theses supported by all sixteenth-century reformers, firmly stressed the opposing theses as, for example, in the discussion of salvation through faith or works, or the sacrifice of the cross and the Mass, of the collegial ministry and the papacy, of the Church invisible and the Roman Catholic Church. Today they are inclined to think that Catholicism "renewed in the spirit of the Council" is in a position to effect the synthesis.

We believe their evaluation is both true and full of promise. Provided that it is not rigidly systematized, it seems to us consistent with the history of recent centuries and with the thought of the Council itself, which is indeed "a first decisive attempt of the Catholic Church to prepare itself for visible unity with other Christian communions." Furthermore, this evaluation seems to us happily to highlight a power always evident in Catholicism, one of whose chief characteristics is, in fact, a spirit of synthesis, a world-embracing and all-including trend which has been operative ever since the beginning in widely different areas, toward a higher unity in Jesus Christ, the first and total object of our faith.

Lastly and above all what we shall cherish from this commentary is precisely the faith to which it testifies and which, transcending the differences that remain in "the personal and supernatural revelation of God through his Word," this faith so clear, so pure, so total in the Word of God who is "the living Christ." Complete and fully visible union can be sought on no other foundation; and by way of compensation, on such a foundation union can rightly be expected.

Henri de Lubac, S.J.

A DAY AT
THE COUNCIL

In our Roman apartment close to the Piazza Venezia, noise from the big thoroughfares is stopped by the sturdy walls of the old dwelling. Moreover, our windows open on an inner court. True, we never see the sun, but living in the midst of the constant traffic in the heart of a big city, lack of light is preferable to constant din.

Midnight sounds from the neighboring belfry. This is the hour that marks the end of one day and the beginning of another day which is also God's today. While falling asleep, it is good to know that at the center of this great city the Christian, the presence of God, is in the midst of men who are numerous and near.

A little oratory has been arranged at the center of our apartment. It opens onto the corridor. If, during the night, there is a moment of wakefulness, what could be more refreshing, more restful than to rediscover prayer and meditation with Christ.

Dawn cannot be seen from our windows. But it is then that we all come together for morning prayer because in addition to the two observer brothers, there are always several brothers who come in turn to live in Rome during the Council, to take care of hospitality or to do the urgent and indispensable work of the secretariat.

After morning prayer, which is the same that is said by our brothers at Taizé or in the fraternities, we have breakfast. This is one of the few moments, not to say the only moment, when we find ourselves again with our brothers. We can make plans for the day, work at a program, learn which bishops will come for the noonday meal or for supper.

Then it is time to leave for the Council. When crossing the bridge, there is almost always a moment of heart-filling joy. The sky widens about the Castel San Angelo, a sky that is all sunshine and brightness. As soon as we reach the basilica, encounters begin. First we go to a side chapel to join the many bishops who, long before the opening of the congregation, have come to pray together in silence. This is also characteristic of those who are waiting for God under the conciliar vault. Then we move toward the observers' tribune where every day new contacts are made or begun. We hurry to our places. The whole conciliar assembly is united in eucharistic prayer.

This is a powerful period of the day. Together we invoke the Holy Spirit on the whole conciliar assembly; together we ask God to come to the help of his people; together we stand around the real presence of Christ in the eucharist; together we venerate the mystery of this presence in our midst and prepare ourselves to listen to what the Lord says to the Church.

How often have we come to this prayer troubled by some event, some word, some attitude, and in this prayer in common once again we have been able to find the peace of Christ.

To say that we are always and in the same way attentive to every intervention would not be true. But our attention was intense when under the dome of St. Peter we listened to a bishop who stated firmly and truthfully things that are going to concern the future and that touch upon our own dominant preoccupation—the problem of the presence of the Christian in the contemporary world.

How often did we not recall some great figure of Christian history, especially that of John XXIII who is now interceding in the communion of saints. How often did we not recall the figure of Martin Luther, telling ourselves that if this man were here, he could not help rejoicing because what was deepest in him, his most essential and purest intentions, were being answered today?

Leaving the Council through the gate of St. Martha, we meet with men whom we love and with whom we share our most pressing preoccupations. Before the gate the cars are waiting. It is possible to prolong for a few moments the lines of a declaration or our impressions of a debate.

Then we have to find those with whom we had made appointments and bring them with us to our apartment and to the noonday meal. By means of conversation at table and breaking the same bread, we who cannot communicate at the same table are given a kind of prefiguration of what will one day be offered us in the visible unity of the one eucharist.

It is so true that the eucharist is the source and at the same time the crown of all unity that men who are constantly subject to the forces of separation and disassociation and are given in the eucharist a supernatural means of living the vocation to unity! It is so true that the eucharist is, for those who receive it with faith and a docile heart, the power that brings about a process of unity!

At the meal different topics are discussed, depending on whether our guests are Asians, South Americans, North Americans, or Africans. It is good to listen to, and hear, different concerns and to receive them for our meditation on ecumenism. The meals are simple but sometimes very pleasant. Frequently, they close in our little oratory with a silent prayer or the "Our Father."

Once our guests have gone, there is a moment of relaxation and silence; then the many interviews begin again. The men who come and go differ one from the other. We are only five to welcome them. At the close of the afternoon we must often accept an invitation from a seminary to discuss some aspect of the ecumenical vocation.

Then it's an often hurried return through crowded streets to meet again in common prayer, to welcome other bishops to our evening meal. We spend much of the evening around the table.

Inserted into this life of community and contacts, work con-

nected with conciliar debates is never missing. We have to follow the evolution of the texts, prepare notes, present our point
of view each time we are asked. Thus our interest was con-
centrated on the elaboration of certain Constitutions: Revelation, Liturgy, The Church in the World Today, and on the
Decree on Ecumenism. This latter plus the texts on revelation
and the contemporary Church seems to us to be the documents
that will do the most to hasten the movement toward the
visible unity of Christians.

Here we would like to present our commentary on the Constitution on Divine Revelation, which will be called upon to
play a considerable role in the ecumenical dialogue between
separated Christians because it attempts to restore a common
language, the language of the Bible, as the expression of the
new foundation of our common faith. But this rediscovered
tongue cannot remain hermetic, and be reserved exclusively
for the initiated. If Christians find once more a common biblical language to speak among themselves of their faith in divine
revelation, they should also try together to find a common
language so that the Church in the world of this time can
proclaim to all men, agnostics and believers, that the life was
manifested by Christ, and in this true life each man may find
complete joy.

If our effort was directed first of all to this text on revelation, it was because it seemed to us to be a useful basis for a
dialogue between Christians and with all men. It is also a text
susceptible to other developments and for this reason it is
useful today when so many problems are raised in biblical
exegesis and hermeneutics. With this conciliar text we wish
to remain open to all these problems so that we can find the
solutions that the Spirit wants to offer the Church in the
modern world.

The study of the text on revelation cannot distract anyone
from the concerns of the man of today. It does not distract us;
on the contrary, it invites us in an early stage of our thinking
after the Council to approach the text on the Church in the

modern world. Revelation—the world, this was the movement
of the Council; this should be the dynamism of our thinking—
to move from dialogue with God to the lot of mankind, with
all men, whether they be believers or agnostics.

During our last audience with Pope John XXIII, he said to
us: "To prepare my decisions, I dialogue with God, simply,
humbly. . . ." We know what doors to the world such dialogue opened. Pope Paul VI continues this dialogue with all,
in the faith and perseverance of a man of God. Dialogue with
God constrains us irresistably to dialogue with all men, since
the God whom we contemplate is he who one day willed to
become man. According to the text that we are going to
comment upon: "For the words of God, expressed in human
tongues, became similar to human language, just as formerly
the Word of the eternal Father, assuming flesh with its human
weakness, became similar to man."

We present, first of all, our commentary on each of the six
chapters of the Constitution, and then Father George H.
Tavard's translation of the Latin text. The length of each
chapter depends on the ecumenical importance of the subjects
treated because it is from this point of view that we have
studied this Constitution.

PROLOGUE

1. The Council and Revelation

The first two words of the Dogmatic Constitution on Revelation immediately give the spirit of this important text of Vatican II: *Dei Verbum, The Word of God.* The Council did not intend to speak of revelation as the transmission of eternal truths by an unchangeable God to an institutional Church. To be sure, revelation does include eternal truths—certainly God is unchangeable, and the Church is an institution—but it was the Council's intention to leave aside a vocabulary that is overly static and notional to adopt deliberately language that is dynamic and alive. Revelation is considered throughout this magnificent text as the living Word that the living God addresses to a living Church composed of living members.

From the very beginning the Council placed itself in a position to listen and to proclaim. The Word of God should be listened to with piety and proclaimed with assurance. The citation of St. John (cf. 1 John 1, 2-3) stresses the dynamic character of the Word of God which is the proclamation of a life, eternal life, of Christ our life who was with the Father and who appeared in time. The apostles saw and heard this Word because it was made flesh and they declared that through this Word a living communion would be established between men and between men and God, the Father and the Son, in the Holy Spirit. The whole text on revelation is dominated by the fundamental evangelical themes of word, life, and communion. The Word of God is the living Christ, whom God

11

gives men to establish between him and them, and among
themselves, the communion of the Spirit in the Church.

The Council of Vatican II tries to be guided by the direc-
tives of the Councils of Trent and Vatican I, but if it carries
them further, it is because these two Councils were not able
to give to the difficult problem of revelation the solution for
which Christians had been waiting since the Reform of the
sixteenth century. Nor can one expect Vatican II to provide
answers to all questions. Will such an answer ever be given
before the eternal Word will enlighten us all in the Kingdom
of God? Many more conciliar sessions will be needed before
all reunited Christians can subscribe to the same doctrine of
revelation. Even so, the text of the Council of Vatican II marks
a decisive advance and contains the first answer to various
questions of the Protestant Reform on this subject.

The Council's intention was not limited to dialogue with
all Christians. If it tried to express the authentic doctrine on
divine revelation and how it is handed on, this was not only
to bring greater clarity to the faith of Catholic Christians, or
to offer the outline of an ecumenical solution to Christians
who were still divided, but it is also and above all that the
Word of God confided to the Church might be heard throughout the whole world, and might call all men to salvation so
that, by hearing it, they may be led to faith, and that faith
might produce in them hope, and hope may unite them in
love. The Prologue of the Constitution closes with the question from St. Augustine about the missionary intention of the
Church which receives the living Word of the living God only
to share with all men the marvelous communion of faith, hope,
and love. The Word of God is addressed to the Church only
in order to reach the whole world. Revelation, the Word of
God, life, and communion in Christ and the Spirit are not only
for Christians, they are for all men.

I
REVELATION

2. Nature and Object of Revelation

Here again it is not a question of defining the nature of revelation according to the intellectual truths it contains and hands on to the Church; here is no trace of a notional or dogmatic concept of revelation. It is essentially the revelation of God himself, the revelation of Father, Son and Spirit, a revelation that is living and personal, a revelation, too, of the will of God. God reveals himself and makes known the mystery of his will. In the measure in which men learn to know the mystery of the will of God, they have access to the Father, through Christ, the Word made flesh and in the Holy Spirit. Revelation is then not an intellectual demonstration of truths to be accepted by reason; it is a personal contact of God with man to whom he makes himself known by bringing man into the mystery of his will, the will of salvation through Christ and in the Holy Spirit. To reveal himself to man, God does not explain himself as the Supreme Being, but he enters in communion with him in the history of Jesus Christ, the Word made flesh, enlightened by the Holy Spirit. Thus, revelation is not considered here as a teaching of doctrines, but as a personal encounter of God the Father with man in the earthly life of Christ and in the hidden life of the Spirit, the mystery of his will. The nature of revelation is therefore essentially personal and historic.

The object of revelation is the union of man with God in a life of communion. There again, this union is not considered as a relationship of minds, between the reason of man and the Being of God, but as a participation of the whole man in the divine nature, as a communion of living persons. Thus, revelation appears as a conversation of the invisible God with men. The text stresses this aspect of revelation as a living conversation of God with men, whom he treats as friends. There is a quotation from the book of Exodus (33, 11) where it is said that "the Lord used to speak with Moses face to face, as one man speaks to another." The friendly character of revelation adds something to the personal and historic aspect already stressed and enables us to see revelation as a living relation with God—Father, Son, and Spirit—and the whole man. God enters into conversation with men according to the text from Baruch (3, 37-38): ". . . he has traced out all the way of understanding, and has given her to Jacob, his servant, to Israel, his beloved son. Since then she has appeared on earth, and moved among men."

In this conversation between God and men, as between two friends, God invites man to a community of life with him and receives him in this communion. The object of revelation is essentially this friendly dialogue between God who invites and receives and man who hears the invitation and enters into the living community with God.

After having explained the nature of revelation, which is personal and historic, and the object of revelation, which is the friendly dialogue and living community between God and man, the text of the Constitution shows briefly how this revelation takes place. The economy of revelation, that is, its organic ensemble includes God's words and actions. We must note once more the insistence on the living and total character of revelation: it is not only a collection of truths and doctrines transmitted to the intelligence, it takes place in the actions and words closely connected with one another and which possess man's whole being. God's acts in the history of salvation manifest and confirm the doctrine and the realities signified by the words; the words announce God's acts in history and explain the mystery that the acts proclaim. Revelation, then, is basically the history of salvation accomplished by God in favor of men, during which he performs acts and pronounces words which throw light on each other: God's works concretize his words, and his words illumine his works. Revelation is a complete history, the history of salvation, not an exposition of doctrines, and it affects man in his whole nature, soul and body.

It is Christ in revelation who is the deepest truth about God and man's salvation; it is he who is the fullness of revelation, and it is through him, the mediator, that it reaches us in its totality. Because he is the Word of God made flesh, Christ is therefore the summary of all that God wants to say to man; he is also the only one who can give us full light about revelation.

3. Preparation for the Revelation of the Gospel

This paragraph discusses the problem of the preparation of total revelation in the Gospel of Christ. The text distinguishes different stages: a certain revelation in creation, the manifestation of God to the first human beings, the initial promise of redemption after the original fall, the providence of God for all men, the vocation of Abraham, the education of the people of Israel, the awaiting of the Messiah, which finally ended in Christ and the Gospel.

The first stage concerns what is usually called natural revelation. This point, often argued in dialogue between Catholic and Protestant theologians, is approached in the light of St. Paul (cf. Rom. 1, 19-20), in a way that dispels difficulties. In fact, there is no question here of a knowledge of God that man could have by way of nature alone, but of the testimony that God gives of himself in creation without specifying whether man can discover this by natural light alone. We will find at the end of this chapter another note about this that comes from Vatican I. But here the stress is on the fact of natural revelation beginning with God and not on the question whether man, by natural light can attain to a knowledge of God. Because God, who creates and conserves all things by his Word, by uttering his Word, by the pre-existing Son, offers in creatures a continuing testimony about himself, creation speaks of God by its very existence, by its beauty, by its perfection. But if this natural revelation, or as the text says, this testimony of God is an objective fact, because of the work of creation and conservation of the Word of God, it is not said here that man can perceive it naturally without the supernatural revelation of the Word of God.

The text even seems to indicate the insufficient character of this testimony to God in creation even for men before the fall. In fact, the second stage of preparation for the Gospel revelation is the manifestation of God in person to our first parents. Creation even in the state of man's unfallen nature does not suffice to reveal God to him. God must manifest himself personally and individually to open the way to transcendent salvation. To raise man towards communion with the personal God, creation, and the testimony to God which it gives are not enough, even for man before the fall. God manifests his transcendent Person and calls man to communion with him in a particular and direct revelation.

After the first fall, God introduces a third stage of his revelation. He lifts up the first parents in the hope of salvation by promising them redemption. This is the promise made to the woman whose descendant will crush the head of the serpent, the symbol of evil (cf. Gen. 3, 15).

God does not abandon his creatures, even his fallen creatures, and the text indicates the fourth stage, the creator's constant care of men, in his vigilant providence. Much more, he wants to give eternal life to all those who seek salvation along the path of moral obedience, of constancy in good works, as St. Paul has written: "[He] . . . will render to every man according to his works. Life indeed will he give to those who by patience in good works seek glory and honor and immortality . . ." (Rom. 2, 6-7).

But the decisive stages of revelation are the vocation of Abraham, the establishment of the People of God, and their messianic expectations. Through the patriarchs, Moses, and the prophets, God taught his chosen People to know him in person. He revealed himself explicitly as the one, living, and true God; this is Judaic monotheism. He also revealed himself as the Father who would take care of his People and who would pronounce just judgments on them; he is the God who entered history and who lived this history with men. Lastly, at the close of all these stages, which were preparatory to the total revelation, we find the promise and the expectation of the Messiah, the Savior of the chosen people and of all men. The messianic prophets brought the People of God to the threshold of the Gospel revelation. God, in these different stages, prepared the way for the Gospel, the supreme, total, and definitive revelation that Christ himself would bring, proclaim, and live among men.

4. Christ Who Brings Revelation to Perfection

Christ's days on earth were the last times of revelation. God had spoken personally to his people by means of the prophets; in the time of the Gospel he came himself in his Son to bring revelation to perfection (cf. Heb. 1, 1-2). The text of the Dogmatic Constitution never ceases insisting on the personal and living character of revelation, thus avoiding any thinking about revelation along the lines of dogmatic intellectualism—in order to show it as the living Word of the personal God who came into history to dialogue with men and bring them into community of life with him.

God has spoken personally in the history of his People through the prophets; he comes, in these last days to speak personally in his Son. He who is the very Word of God comes to dwell among men to disclose to them the final mysteries of God. God no longer speaks here through men; his Word made flesh becomes a man to live in the midst of men, to speak directly to them and thus to perfect the work of salvation. He who sees Christ sees the Father (cf. John 14, 9) and this is how he perfects revelation because he himself is the total revelation of God through his personal presence among men by all that he said and did but especially by his death and resurrection and finally his sending the Holy Spirit. The definitive content of this revelation is summed up in the testimony of Christ that God is with us in person, that he frees us from sin and death, and that he raises us for eternal life.

Christ, in thus establishing a new and definitive alliance with man, put an end to all public revelation of God. The revelation of God to his People is complete, and no further public revelation is to be expected. The possibility is allowed that God might address a private revelation to a Christian, for example, in a vision, but this revelation cannot concern all people and their salvation. Before Christ's glorious return at the end of time, there will then be no new public revelation because the Gospel is the definitive revelation of God in this world for the salvation of men.

5. Revelation Should Be Received in Faith

This paragraph is one of the most remarkable and most unexpected in the Constitution on Revelation. In fact, according to the usual pattern of explanation of Catholic theology, one might expect to find here a paragraph on the Church receiving and handing on revelation and then only a paragraph on the personal faith which accepts revelation. The change of sequence is indeed indicative of the spirit of the Council and very important for the ecumenical dialogue. Certainly the role of the Church in the transmission of revelation is not neglected; we shall see that this important point is developed in

Chapter II. But that the acceptance of personal faith should be situated in the first place in this Constitution reveals one of the newest perspectives for Catholicism since the sixteenth century. Fear, justified or not, of subjectivism and of free examination had accustomed the Catholic Church to speak of the acceptance of revelation in terms of submission to authority rather than in terms of personal faith. The Council, free from an apologetic or polemic attitude to Protestantism, first, states very simply how personal faith accepts God's revelation and second, explains how the Church hands on this revelation.

This acceptance of revelation by man is described as a profoundly personal act: "To God who reveals himself is due the 'obedience of faith.'" The text speaks of revelation not as the totality of truths that must be accepted, but as the person of God in his act of revelation whom man meets in his act of faith. Three different times the text insists on the personal character of revelation: in one sentence we find twice the expression "to God who reveals himself," and once, "the revelation he has made." The obedience of faith is considered as a free act of man. By faith a man does not submit himself blindly to an authority that constrains him, even if this be the authority of God. It is true that man surrenders himself totally to God, but it is in freely offering him the obedience of faith and in willingly adhering to revelation. The text insists on the free character of faith through which man offers himself, surrenders, and adheres to God who reveals himself. Finally, the obedience of faith is the offering of the whole man. It does not consist only in the adherence of the reason to revealed truths, it leads the whole man with his intelligence and his will to surrender himself to God. The text insists on the plenary character of faith. Man surrenders himself totally (*se totum*), offering God a total homage (*plenum obsequium*) of intelligence and will. Thus, in a single sentence, the first in this paragraph, the Constitution shows clearly the personal, free, and plenary character of the act of faith.

This personal, free, and plenary faith is a fruit of God's grace, which precedes the act of faith and sustains it, coming before and assisting it. Faith needs the inner help of the Holy Spirit. It is through him that the heart is animated and turned towards the contemplation of God. Without this secret action of the Holy Spirit in the heart, man cannot begin to move and be converted to God, nor can faith be born, through which alone man adheres voluntarily to the revelation given by God. The Holy Spirit opens the eyes of man's mind and gives him the joy of adhering to, and believing in, the truth. Finally, the Holy Spirit acts so as to make faith perfect and thus, to deepen the understanding of revelation.

This whole passage on the role of grace and the Holy Spirit in the birth of faith, conversion of heart, openness of mind, the gift of joy, a deeper understanding of revelation, has a most ecumenical character. Protestants who are accustomed to this kind of explanation will be well aware that this conciliar text marks a convergence of theological ideas about the acceptance of revelation by personal faith, the fruit of grace, and the work of the Holy Spirit in the heart.

6. Revealed Truths

This paragraph considers once again the question of natural revelation according to St. Paul (cf. Rom. 1, 20), not only from the point of view of God who reveals himself, as in section three, but also from the point of view of the knowledge man might have of this natural revelation. Here one is aware that Vatican II wished to be in accord with the texts of Vatican I. Yet care must be taken to notice the order in which the texts of Vatican I are cited. If these texts lack the biblical tonality of the texts of Vatican II, the order in which they are presented reveals the intention of Vatican II to begin with God and to look at the whole of revelation, rather than to begin with reason and to examine once again whether man can really know the true God in the light of natural revelation without biblical revelation.

The paragraph begins by reaffirming the personal character of divine revelation in which God manifests and communicates himself as well as his eternal plan for the salvation of men. Then comes the first quotation from Vatican I (Constitution, *Dei Filius,* Chapter II, "De revelatione"). But it should be noted that this quotation is taken from the end of the second paragraph which is, as it were, the conclusion of the perspective of Vatican I on the relation between natural and supernatural revelation. While Vatican I starts from natural revelation and the possibility of knowing God according to the light of reason in order to arrive at the consideration of the necessity for supernatural revelation, Vatican II begins with the personal revelation of God and of salvation, quoting, at the beginning, the close of the development of Vatican I. The perspective is in some way reversed.

God wished to manifest himself and to communicate himself, as well as his plan of salvation, "that they may participate in the divine wealth, which utterly exceeds the human mind's comprehension" (quotation from Vatican I). And Vatican I ended the paragraph with a text from St. Paul: "Eye has not seen, nor ear heard, nor has it entered into the heart of man, what things God has prepared for those who love him" (1 Cor. 2, 9). Vatican II therefore begins where Vatican I stopped: at the problem of the relation between supernatural and natural revelation. The perspective of Vatican II seems more biblical and theocentric; it begins with the personal revelation of God and goes forward to meet man and his possible knowledge of God. Vatican II affirms in the first place the necessity of the personal revelation of God so that man can share in the divine goods that totally surpass the comprehension of his mind.

Only then appears, in the text of Vatican II, the question of natural revelation from the point of view of the knowledge that man can have of it. This is where there is agreement with the thought of Vatican I, but, as we have said, in reverse perspective. Vatican II then quotes the beginning of the first paragraph of Chapter II, "De revelatione," of Vatican I and accepts it as its own; it also confesses with St. Paul (Rom. 1, 20): "God, the beginning and end of all things, may be known with certainty by the natural light of human reason reflecting on created things."

This sentence echoes the thought of St. Paul when writing to the Romans: "For since the creation of the world his invisible attributes are clearly seen—his everlasting power also and divinity—being understood through the things that are made. And so they are without excuse seeing that, although they knew God, they did not glorify him as God or give thanks but became vain in their reasonings and their senseless minds have been darkened" (Rom. 1, 20-21). Certainly then, it is possible to know the power and eternity of God through reflecting on creation. It is this sure possibility that makes it inexcusable for man not to recognize God and not to pay him worship when he may be known through his works, even though he is invisible. Man, then, cannot hide behind the excuse that he has not received the gift of faith to know God and to pray to him. The permanent testimony to God in creation accuses man of sin when he does not recognize God as principle and end of all things by the natural light of human reason, beginning with created realities, because the eternal power of God is knowable through creation, and this elementary knowledge ought to lead man to give praise and thanks. The purpose of these remarks is to exclude a materialistic concept, namely, that the world would not speak of God, and religion would be a purely personal affair. The world is not autonomous in relation to God because in spite of sin, creation remains linked with its Creator who gives witness to himself in his works, who remains knowable through human reason, at least in his eternal existence and creative power, and who thus leaves man without excuse for not knowing God and worshipping him, without excuse even if he does not have the grace of faith and can use only his natural reason.

Yet after repeating what Vatican I says about natural revelation, Vatican II immediately quotes another passage from Vatican I on the necessity of supernatural revelation for knowledge, "with firm certainty and without error," of those things that are not of themselves inaccessible to natural man. After affirming that certain divine realities are knowable by human reason beginning with reflection on creation, Vatican II, like Vatican I, recalls that revelation is necessary not only to know what is not knowable in the order of God through human reason alone, but for what in the actual condition of the human race all can know easily and with firm certitude, free from any admixture of error, the divine realities which of themselves are not inaccessible to human reason.

Thus, this possibility of a natural knowledge of God, necessary for the exclusion of a materialistic idea of the autonomy of the world and the idea of a religion which would be a purely private affair, becomes relative when it is considered in the light of supernatural revelation. Of themselves certain things of the divine order are not inaccessible to human reason. It is inherent in creation itself (*per se*), because of the faithfulness of God's witness that these divine realities are not inaccessible; it is because God had no part in sin and did not break with his creation that he is still knowable in it and through human reason. But it must be noted that the negative turn of the phrase already relativizes the possibility of a natural theology: *"per se impervia non sunt"*—these divine realities are not inaccessible of themselves.

This possible natural theology is relativized by still other considerations, all of which make supernatural revelation a necessary illumination for natural revelation. There is the actual condition of the human race, permeated by sin, which makes this knowledge of God by reason difficult; all cannot attain it; it is not an easy thing; certitude about it is not firm;

error has crept in. Thus, because of all these circumstances supernatural revelation brings an indispensable strength to the natural revelation of things, which by themselves are not inaccessible to human reason. Thanks to supernatural revelation, "in the present condition of mankind, the divine realities, which are not in themselves beyond the reach of human reason, may be known by all in a short time, with firm certainty and without error." But, of course, that is not the only purpose of supernatural revelation. As Vatican I said to perfect its development about the necessity of revelation: "It is not for this reason that it must be said that (supernatural) revelation is absolutely necessary, but because God, in his infinite goodness, has ordained man to a supernatural end, that is to say, so that he may participate in the divine wealth, which utterly exceeds the human mind's comprehension." We have seen that Vatican II began its statement with the last words of this sentence.

Therefore, the one idea that will be central in our Dogmatic Constitution, is the one idea of the first five paragraphs of the first chapter—the personal and supernatural revelation of God through his Word.

II

THE TRANSMISSION OF
DIVINE REVELATION

7. The Apostles and Their Successors
the Heralds of the Gospel

The revelation of God, whose goal is the salvation of all men, was not given haphazardly subject to fluctuations of history and human thought. Granted its capital importance, God made sure that his Word would be kept intact through history and so that it might be handed on to all generations. These two intentions of God in regard to his Word were realized in the mandate that he entrusted to the apostles. Christ, having fulfilled the whole revelation of God, charged the apostles to proclaim it to all men. They were the first to be made responsible for the basic task of preserving the deposit of revelation and for its transmission within the Church to all men. This safeguarding of the deposit of the Gospel would eventually establish the boundaries of the writings of the New Covenant—the New Testament; but this fixation of the biblical canon would not render obsolete the need for a transmission of the communication, interpretation, explicitation and application of God's eternal Word.

In this apostolic mandate to preserve and transmit, we see the outline of the two realities whose mutual relations the Constitution is about to describe: Scripture and Tradition. Of course, the Council does not pretend to liken exclusively the preservation intact of revelation to Scripture on one hand and the faithful transmission of this revelation to Tradition on the other. Nevertheless, it seems that this responsibility for preserving the deposit leads in a special way to the formation of the New Testament and the power of handing on the Gospel in the Church constitutes more specially the role of Tradition.

The Gospel, promised by the prophets, was fulfilled and promulgated by Christ's own tongue. He gave the apostles the mission of proclaiming it to all men "as the source of all saving truth and moral discipline." The Gospel of Christ as preached by the apostles is, then, the sole source of truth, and gives us the whole saving truth. This means that we do not have to look for the truth about salvation which would not be found in the Gospel as in its source and that we do not have to look for human truth in the Gospel, but only truth concerning man's salvation. Furthermore, the Gospel is also the source of the discipline of our life; it is the setting where our moral life is formed. The Gospel promulgated by Christ and proclaimed by the apostles is therefore truth and life, the source of saving truth and of all moral life. In this promulgation of the Gospel of truth and life, the apostles communicated to all men the gifts of God himself.

This transmission of the Gospel was first faithfully accomplished by the apostles of Christ. This Gospel contains either what they had received from Christ when he spoke to them, lived with them, acted in their midst, or what they learned from the Holy Spirit who recalled to them all that Christ had said (cf. John 14, 26: *suggerente*). The apostles transmitted the revealed Gospel by oral preaching, for example, by their life and by their doctrinal teaching. In addition, the Gospel was also handed on by the apostles and apostolic men who wrote the saving message under the inspiration of the Holy Spirit—the evangelists and the different authors of the epistles, the Acts of the Apostles, and the Apocalypse.

Furthermore, God provided for the preservation and transmission of his Gospel in the Church after the death of Christ's apostles and New Testament writers. For this reason the apostles prepared their successors, ministers, overseers, and bishops, to whom they handed on their own proper charge of teaching the Gospel. The special purpose of this episcopal responsibility for supervision, entrusted to the apostles was the ceaseless effort to preserve the Gospel intact and to keep it always living in the Church. Here we see again the two aspects of the apostolic mandate about the Word of God, namely, preservation and transmission. Overseers also have this apostolic responsibility of preserving the deposit of truth intact and of faithfully handing it on so that it may live and act in the Church. Scripture will better show the obligation of keeping the Gospel truth intact. Tradition will stress the function of the living transmission of this same truth.

Bishops, like the apostles, should become the guardians of Scripture and the promoters of Tradition. In one and the other it is the same Gospel that is expressed, the single source of all saving truth. This is why the Council can say that Tradition (chronologically first) and Scripture (established later) are like the mirror in which the Church contemplates God, from whom she has received all, and this is true as long as she journeys on earth and until the day when she will reach her goal when she will see God face to face, just as he is. Tradition joined to Scripture—two forms in one Church of the unique Gospel, the sole source of truth and life—is compared to Scripture as to a mirror; that is to say, that God cannot be contemplated in them just as he is, but only in a mirror. As long as the Church has not reached the final goal, she can contemplate God only through signs; she can know the truth only in the mirror of Tradition and Scripture. The figure of the mirror and the Church's journey on earth show that in the contemplation of God and the knowledge of the truth, all is not revealed at once, in full light, face to face. The Church has to journey until the day when she will see God as he is; she has to try to discern ever more clearly God's truth in the mirror of Tradition joined to Scripture. This mirror reflects from the beginning the whole saving truth, but the Church ought to study it in ever greater profundity, with an ever more sustained attention, discovering all its implications until the day when the mirror will give place to light, face to face.

8. Holy Transmission

The preaching of the apostles is presented in a special manner in the inspired books of Scripture; but even before the canon of the New Testament was established, the intention of preserving and continuing the Gospel teaching was present in the Church and in the minds of the apostles. They can be seen exhorting the faithful to guard what had been handed on to them, which was what they themselves had received from Christ and the Holy Spirit. This tradition was communicated to the faithful by word of mouth or letter (cf. Thess. 2, 15); their faith was handed on once and for all and they had to fight in its defense (cf. Jude 3).

Here, let us attempt in a parenthesis, as it were, to understand the meaning given to the word "Tradition." The Council does not circumscribe its meaning in a sentence of the Constitution. It is throughout the whole of Chapter II that the notion of Tradition gradually becomes more exact and defined. It is possible that the Council would have found it difficult to reach an agreement about a clear-cut definition. So it is necessary to grapple with the problem of understanding just what the Council meant by "Tradition" each time it uses the word. An explanatory note containing a correction presented for the vote of the fourth period of the Council tells us that if instead of "This living Tradition" were inserted the words "This Tradition stemming from the apostles," which comes from St. Irenaeus, the purpose would be to show more clearly that here it is a question of the divine origin of Tradition and not of purely ecclesiastical traditions.[1] When the Council speaks of Tradition, it wishes to refer to Tradition as the transmission

[1] *Adv. Haer.*, III, 3, 2.

of the Gospel of Christ by the apostles and their successors; it does not mean ecclesiastical traditions insofar as they are habits and customs inherited from history.

Nevertheless, it would have been useful had the Council given definitions that could throw light on the meaning of the text, as the Fourth World Conference on Faith and Order did at Montreal in 1963; the Report of Section II in fact said: "We have distinguished between several meanings of the word tradition. We speak of *Tradition* (with a capital "T"), of *tradition* (with a small "t"), and of *traditions*. By *Tradition* we mean *the Gospel itself,* handed on from generation to generation in and through the Church, Christ himself present in the light of the Church. By *tradition* we mean the *process of tradition.* The term *traditions* is used in two ways: to indicate the diversity of *forms of expression* and of what we call *confessional traditions.*" [2]

According to the Montreal vocabulary, the Council wished to speak of Tradition in the first sense, that of Tradition of divine origin (Vatican II), of the Gospel itself, handed on from generation to generation in and through the Church (Montreal), and not of traditions in the third sense, of purely ecclesiastical traditions (Vatican II), or of forms of expression (Montreal). Yet the Council was not able to avoid speaking of tradition in Montreal's second meaning; that is, the process of tradition; the expression of tradition recovers therefore in the conciliar text the idea of Tradition of divine origin (the Gospel transmitted) and the notion of the process of living Tradition (the transmission of the Gospel). Some Council Fathers foresaw the difficulty of this double meaning and asked at the fourth period that the expression "living Tradition" be restored where there had been substituted "Tradition stemming from the apostles." Two noted the confusion that might result from using the word "Tradition" sometimes in an active sense (the process of living tradition: the transmission of the Gos-

[2] Final Report, Fourth World Conference on Faith and Order, Sec. II, no. 39. (Eng. trans. available.)

pel), sometimes in a passive sense (the content of divine Tradition: the Gospel transmitted). The answer was given that
the two senses are intimately linked and that the meaning
should be determined by the context. For example, when the
text says: "What has been transmitted by the apostles contains . . ." the meaning is "passive" and concerns the content
of Tradition.

It is true that it is difficult to distinguish absolutely between
the content of divine Tradition from its process of living transmission. Nevertheless, it is sometimes a delicate task to interpret the expression "tradition" according to the context. Yet
it should be recognized that too sharp a definition would perhaps have hardened positions. We later will see why it might
have been better to keep an organic and dynamic idea of Tradition rather than revive opposing schools.

Yet to us, it seems useful to state precisely the different
meanings of the notion of tradition so that afterwards we can
distinguish more clearly how the Council uses it in different
contexts:

(1) *Apostolic Tradition* is the whole evangelical message
just as the apostles, having received it from Christ and the
New Testament authors under the inspiration of the Holy
Spirit entrusted it to the Church to be guarded and transmitted until the end of time; this apostolic Tradition is expressed
in a special manner in the inspired books of the New Testament, and it is brought into the living Tradition of the
Church, in its dogmas, sacraments, and sanctified life.

(2) *Living Tradition in the Church* is the totality of dogmas, sacraments, and holiness of the Church in the act of the
transmission of faith; the Tradition, from the apostles and
the inspired writers, guards and transmits the apostolic Tradition that it carries; living Tradition in this sense is both apostolic Tradition (the revealed content of what is transmitted)
and the process of tradition (the transmission of the revealed
content). It is, we think, in this sense that includes content

and process that the Council speaks most frequently of tradition.

(3) *The tradition of the Gospel* is the act or process by which the apostolic Tradition, the Gospel, is transmitted in and through the Church; this act or process of transmission includes preaching, liturgy, catechesis, theology, mission, witness, and life of the Church.

(4) *Ecclesiastical traditions* are the forms of expression that the transmission of the Gospel takes according to places, times, and cultures in order to best attain its goal, which is the communication of the Word of God to men to lead them to faith, hope, and charity.

These definitions cover those of Montreal and enable us to see that the Council speaks most often of Tradition in the second sense.

What was transmitted by the apostles is then defined by the Council. This "contains all that leads to the sanctification of the life of the People of God and to the growth of faith." The text does not specify what are "all" these realities that Tradition includes; it insists rather on its active character, which leads the People of God to live in a holy way and increases its faith. Tradition here appears as a life, a dynamism of faith that grows and deepens. Tradition is the very life of the holy Church in faith: "The Church, in her doctrine, life and worship, perpetuates and transmits to all generations all that she is and all that she believes." Here Tradition is identified with the total life of the Church (doctrine, existence, worship); Tradition perpetuates and transmits the whole life and the entire faith. This is a vital and dynamic conception of Tradition, which is the life of the Gospel of Christ in the Church under the form of doctrinal teaching, of sanctified living, of sacramental worship insofar as they assure the continuity and bring about the transmission of the very being of the Church and her faith. Tradition is the life of the faith of the Church which now continues and transmits itself. All the ways through which we try to explain the nature of Tradition, according to the Council, are only approximations because of its vital and dynamic character. Happily this character was stressed by the Council.

The Fourth World Conference on Faith and Order at Montreal in 1963 expressed a similar concept of Tradition and it is good to emphasize this ecumenical convergence between the theologians of the Council and those of the ecumenical Conference (Protestants, Anglicans, Old Catholics, Orthodox): "In our present situation, we wish to reconsider the problem of Scripture and Tradition, or rather, that of Tradition and Scripture. And therefore we wish to propose the following statement as a fruitful way of reformulating the question. Our starting point is that we are all living in a Tradition which goes back to our Lord and has its roots in the Old Testament, and are all indebted to that Tradition inasmuch as we have received the revealed truth, the Gospel, through its being transmitted from one generation to another. Thus we can say that we exist as Christians by the Tradition of the Gospel (the *paradosis* of the *kerygma*) testified in Scripture, transmitted in and by the Church through the power of the Holy Spirit. Tradition taken in this sense is actualized in the preaching of the Word, in the administration of the sacraments and worship, in Christian teaching and theology, and in mission and witness to Christ by the lives of the members of the Church. What is transmitted in the process of tradition is the Christian faith, not only as a sum of tenets, but as a living reality transmitted through the operation of the Holy Spirit. We can speak of the Christian Tradition (with a capital "T"), whose content is God's revelation and self-giving in Christ, present in the life of the Church." [3]

As Vatican II, Montreal insists on Tradition inasmuch as it is "a living, transmitted reality" whose content is the "revelation of God, the gift that he makes of himself in Christ, his presence in the life of the Church." The Church transmits

[3] *Ibid.*, Sec. II, nos. 45-46.

this Tradition by preaching, sacraments, worship, teaching, theology, mission, witnessing, and life. Vatican II puts it more briefly: "in her doctrine, life and worship."

This Tradition, which comes from the apostles, and which is the living Gospel in the Church, the continual transmission of the being and faith of the Church, progresses (*proficit*) under the assistance of the Holy Spirit. We must clearly understand the words used here. First we must comment on the term "the assistance of the Holy Spirit." Assistance is not inspiration. Only the apostles and the biblical writers are considered by the Church as having been inspired in their transmission of the Word of God. The Church does not enjoy inspiration in its Tradition, but the assistance of the Holy Spirit. This means that the living Tradition of the Church cannot add a revealed truth, under the inspiration of the Spirit, to what was given completely and definitively by the apostles in their oral and written tradition, and by the writers of the New Testament, who alone enjoyed the inspiration of the Holy Spirit. Revelation was achieved by the apostles and New Testament writers under the inspiration of the Holy Spirit.

The assistance of the Holy Spirit enables the Church to deepen revelation and to develop its implications, but not to add to this revelation truths which were not found there from apostolic Tradition or from the writing of the New Testament. Thus, the Church, in its Tradition, only discovers again and deepens under the assistance of the Holy Spirit what was given once and for all in the Tradition of the apostles and consigned by writing in the New Testament. When our text says, then, that "The Tradition that issues from the apostles progresses in the Church," allusion is made to this deepening of revelation and the developing of its implications, which takes place in the living Tradition of the Church, under the assistance of the Holy Spirit. There is no question of development by the quantitative addition of new truths but of an organic growth of the awareness of the Church which understands always more deeply the whole truth which was given once and for all under the inspiration of the Holy Spirit by the Tradition of the apostles and consigned to Scripture.

This organic growth of the understanding by the Church in regard to revelation contained in apostolic Tradition cannot bring the Church to contradict in any way whatsoever the original deposit of revelation which was entrusted to the Church through the apostles. Here in a footnote Vatican II recalls Vatican I to make very clear how the "development" of Tradition in the Church is to be understood: "For the doctrine of faith which God has revealed has not been proposed, like a philosophical invention, to be perfected by human ingenuity; but has been delivered as a divine deposit to the Spouse of Christ, to be faithfully kept and infallibly declared. Hence, also, that meaning of the sacred dogmas is perpetually to be retained which our holy Mother the Church has once declared; nor is that meaning ever to be departed from, under the pretense or pretext of a deeper comprehension of them."

One notes immediately the difference of perspective in the two Vatican Councils. Vatican I wants to defend the immutability of faith, confronting all the evolutionary and scientistic tendencies: faith should not change because science evolves. It is indeed the meaning of the canon referring to this paragraph: "If anyone shall assert it to be possible that sometimes, according to the progress of science, a sense is to be given to doctrines propounded by the Church different from that which the Church has understood and understands, let him be anathema."

The perspective of Vatican II is entirely different. On the contrary, there is a desire to affirm the possibility of a development of Tradition in the Church. This concept, if poorly understood, could imply that Tradition makes a quantitative addition of truths to the revealed deposit transmitted by the apostles. Now it is precisely here that the citation of Vatican I, although making another point, is useful: "For the doctrine of faith which God has revealed has not been proposed, like a philosophical invention, to be perfected by human ingenuity; but has been delivered as a divine deposit to the Spouse of Christ, to be faithfully kept and infallibly declared." The two terms should be compared: *perficienda* of Vatican I and *proficit* of Vatican II. The doctrine of faith cannot be perfected, in the sense of a philosophic discovery, by the addition of elements and for reasons which would be foreign to it (Vatican I); but Tradition develops, in the sense that it goes more and more deeply into the doctrine of faith that God has revealed in an organic and homogeneous growth of the conscious knowledge of the Church, which meditates ceaselessly on the unique revelation transmitted by the apostles (Vatican II).

The verb "to flourish" is found in the quotation that Vatican I takes from St. Vincent of Lerins at the close of the paragraph that we have just quoted to insist on the homogeneity of the increase of faith based on the immutable deposit of revelation. This is also the thought of Vatican II. "Let then the intelligence, science and wisdom of each and all, of individuals and of the whole Church, in all ages and all times, increase and flourish in abundance and vigor; but simply in its own proper kind, that is to say, in one and the same doctrine, one and the same judgment."

These citations have shown that Vatican I was above all preoccupied with the defense of the immutable meaning of dogmas, while Vatican II is careful to show that if revelation is perfect and immutable, Tradition, which brings it, meditates on it, lives it, and transmits it, progresses by the deepening of this revelation and by the development of these implications. But Councils agree that the development of understanding or of Tradition adds nothing to the deposit of revelation, to "the doctrine of faith" (Vatican I), to "apostolic Tradition" (Vatican II).

The rest of the text will show how Vatican II envisages the development of Tradition. It is not apostolic Tradition but "insight into the realities and the words transmitted" that progresses or increases. A correction, substituting "insight" (*perceptio*) for the word "intelligence" (*intelligentia*) was explained in exactly this way: *intelligentia* could be understood as an ablative, this could have led to the translation: ("The Tradition that issues from the apostles) grows by means of intelligence into the realities and into the words transmitted." With the word *perceptio* the subject of the growth is clearly indicated. The explicitation of the correction insists on this in saying that thus, "It clearly appears that development does not affect Tradition itself but only the understanding that one may have of it." It might therefore be asked why the preceding sentence reads: "The Tradition that issues from the apostles progresses in the Church under the assistance of the Holy Spirit." The wording of the earlier text should be remembered: "This living Tradition in the Church progresses under the assistance of the Holy Spirit." This text, before it was corrected, accented the living Tradition in the Church as an act of transmission of revelation and it was not surprising that it was said to progress. But as we have seen, the correction ("The Tradition that issues from the apostles") wished to stress the divine character of Tradition and so the idea of progress had to be minimized because revelation cannot progress, only the understanding that we can have of it. This is another example of the failure to make clear the different meanings of "Tradition." But the insight that this correction and its explanation give us is valuable because it shows us that in the end the Council distinguished within Tradition its unchangeable content (apostolic Tradition) and the insight into what is transmitted, an insight that increases and grows. We again find here united the two elements of what we call "the living Tradition in the Church": (1) unchangeable apostolic Tradition, contained and transmitted; (2) the process of progressive Tradition which contains and transmits. Through these hesitations and corrections the Council clearly shows that it rejects the idea that Tradition in progressing could quantitatively add truths to the deposit of revelation; Tradition issuing from the apostles progresses, not in itself but in the Church, that is to say, in the insight that the Church has into the things and the words transmitted.

How can this insight into Tradition issuing from the apostles grow or increase (*crescit*) in the Church through the assistance of the Holy Spirit? The Council gives several typical ways in which insight into the realities transmitted by Tradition is deepened. It is interesting to note the order in which these ways are set down, especially that it was not until the last edition that mention was made of the magisterium of the hierarchy and this was added in the *modi*. Insight into things and words transmitted by Tradition grows:

(1) Thanks to the contemplation and study by believers (the faithful and theologians) who meditate on these things and these words in their heart like Mary (reference to Luke 2, 19 and 51).

(2) Thanks to the deep understanding of spiritual realities which comes from experiences (the deepening of faith by the experience of Christian life).

(3) Thanks to the preaching of those who have received a certain charism of truth with the succession of the episcopacy.

Understanding of the content of Tradition grows and deepens therefore by means of contemplation, study, the experience of the People of God, and the preaching of the ministers of truth. This continually deepening understanding of revelation transmitted by Tradition guides the Church towards the fullness of truth throughout the centuries until the day when she will contemplate God face to face, and when the Word of God will be totally fulfilled in her.

The Fathers of the Church in their writings testify to the vivifying presence of Tradition. Its riches flow through the concrete existence and profound life of the Church; they penetrate her faith and her prayer. This living and life-giving Tradition, whose presence is noted in the writings of the Fathers, has led the Church to an important decision about its origins. It is, in fact, the apostolic Tradition transmitted in and by the Church that gave her the necessary light to make the decisive choice of the canonical books of the New Testament. Of course this choice was not made in a day, nor was it imposed on the Church suddenly and clearly. It is the apostolic Tradition, present in the heart of the Church and transmitted by her, that little by little enlightened her about the choice to be made. Thus, the Church could discern the apostolic or post-apostolic writings that faithfully reflected the apostolic Tradition that she was handing on from the apostles in her doctrine, life, and worship. Through Tradition the integral canon of the holy books was made known to the Church. The text stresses the supernatural character of this discovery of the canon of the New Testament in making it the subject of the sentence: the canon is made known to the Church by Tradition.

The establishment of the canon therefore was not only a decision of the Church but a supernatural fact which determined the Church by reason of the inspired content of the holy books and of their correspondence with the apostolic Tradition that the Church possessed and handed on from her beginning. The canon of the written Word of God is the subject of this event, of which the Church is the beneficiary and Tradition the providential means.

The fact of the recognition of the New Testament by the Church underlines the decisive role of Tradition. In the ecumenical dialogue it is important once again to consider the role of Tradition and of the Church at the time of the recognition of the New Testament canon.

Moreover, the role of Tradition did not cease with the establishment of the canon. The Council affirms that by Tradition, which preserves revelation in the life of the Church, the sacred texts are more deeply understood by the Church and are constantly kept active in her. The living Tradition in the Church therefore enables her to go deeply into the Word of God contained in Scripture and to give it full efficacy in her life.

The role of Tradition in the formation of Scripture and in their interpretation by the Church was strongly affirmed at the Montreal Conference: "The oral and written tradition of the prophets and apostles under the guidance of the Holy Spirit led to the formation of Scriptures and to the canonization of the Old and New Testaments as the Bible of the Church. The very fact that Tradition precedes the Scriptures points to the significance of Tradition, but also to the Bible as the treasure of the Word of God. For the post-apostolic Church the appeal to the Tradition received from the apostles became the criterion. As this Tradition was embodied in the apostolic writings, it became natural to use those writings as an authority for determining where the true Tradition was to be found. In the midst of all tradition, these early records of divine revelation have a special basic value, because of their apostolic character. But the Gnostic crisis in the second century shows that the mere existence of apostolic writings did not solve the problem. When the canon of the New Testament had been finally defined and recognized by the Church, it was still more natural to use this body of writings as an indispensable criterion. The Tradition in its written form, as Holy Scripture (comprising both the Old and the New Testament), has to be interpreted by the Church in ever new situations . . . The Scriptures as documents can be letter only. It is the Spirit who is the Lord and Giver of life. Accordingly we may say that the right interpretation (taking the words in the widest possible sense) is that interpretation which is guided by the Holy Spirit. But this does not solve the problem of criterion. We arrive at the quest for a hermeneutical principle."[4]

Thus, for the Council, God has certainly spoken in times past and his words are consigned to Scripture, but he never ceases to dialogue with the Church, the Spouse of his Son, through Tradition which explains to her the inspired words of the holy books, enables her to grasp all their depths and dynamic relevance. The Holy Spirit makes the Gospel ring out

[4] *Ibid.*, Sec. II, nos. 42, 49-50, 52.

like a clear voice in the Church and through her in the world; the Holy Spirit guides believers into the whole truth and enables the word of Christ to dwell in them abundantly. Here the living Tradition of the Church is placed in relation with the divine person of the Holy Spirit; it is the Holy Spirit who enlivens Tradition, continues the dialogue between God and the Church, makes the Gospel live, enables believers to grow in the knowledge of truth, and places in their hearts Christ's abundant word.

9. Mutual Relation between Holy Tradition and Holy Scripture

At the beginning of this paragraph it should be remembered that the Council did not try to decide between two theological schools whose positions were at the root of the first big difficulties of the Council and the rejection of the first schema on revelation which was then entitled "Sources of Revelation." John XXIII, it will be recalled, put an end to the impasse by asking that a study be made of the text by a mixed commission (Theological Commission and the Secretariat for Unity) and that the title be changed to "On divine revelation." Before discussion was resumed during the third session, the Commission warned the Council that it did not intend to settle the question on the material sufficiency or insufficiency of Scripture: some believe that all revealed truths are to be found in Scripture, explicitly or implicitly; others think that certain revealed truths are handed on only by Tradition (theory of the "two sources") . But if it was the intention of the Commission not to settle the question that divided the two schools, it must be said that the final text does bring new light that eventually may solve the difficulty and bring the impasse to an end.

The theory known as "the two sources of revelation" (Scripture and Tradition) is missing from the text; if one confines oneself to the Dogmatic Constitution and the interventions which explain it, one cannot say that revealed truths are handed on by Tradition alone, and which Scripture does not contain in any way. Yet Tradition is not assigned a role that is merely interpretative of Scripture. It seems that an advance is being made towards the idea that revelation is found wholly in Scripture and wholly in Tradition, which are therefore not two distinct sources but two conjoined forms, both of which yield the whole revealed truth, the Gospel of Christ, according to modes that are different and proper to each. Thus, without having chosen between the two positions, conciliar reflection has been able to move beyond them to orient theology towards a new solution, which might well be an ecumenical solution capable of uniting divided Christians. Here should be recognized the value of the conciliar confrontation which on this point did not result in a victory for some and a defeat for others, but to an advance beyond old positions by means of an outline of a solution which could easily lead in the future to unhoped for ecumenical fruits.

At this point we touch the mystery of the Council in the Church of Christ, which is a mystery of charity fostering a greater light as a result of a wider and deeper understanding of the truth. Here, majority and minority have not the same meaning that they have in a wordly situation, in spite of exterior appearances and the sin of those men in the Church who always want to block the will of God. If majority and minority are transfigured by supernatural charity, it is true that they enter into a difficult dialogue that is like a painful childbirth and which finally leads them to a new position in which each of the earlier positions dies to be reborn in the dawn of a possible unity. Of course, once the Council is over, each side can try to reclaim its rights and it is then that conciliar vigilance is necessary. Our text on revelation could provide biased minds with arguments that would justify positions whose transcendence has been foreseen and sketched, but it should give confidence to honest theologians who in the spirit of the Council will work energetically to make the most of the positive elements of a text that can guide their thinking toward an ecumenical solution of the problem of the mutual relations of Scripture and Tradition.

The ninth paragraph of the Constitution is important, and we should study it with care. It opens with the affirmation that Tradition and Scripture are interconnected and that they communicate with each other. They constitute a true unity and tend toward the same goal because they flow from the same divine source. Here the text makes very clear that there is only one source of truth, which is the revelation of God, the Gospel of Christ, "formerly promised through the prophets, and now fulfilled and orally proclaimed by himself" (no. 7). Scripture and Tradition should not be considered as two distinct sources of revelation; we should go higher and further than Scripture and Tradition until we come to the Gospel of Christ himself, the Word of God of which they are the first and original forms, the first and primitive manifestations in the Church, authentic channels, profoundly united one to the other, communicating one with the other, both directed to the same goal, namely, the universal knowledge of the Word of God in the Church and through the Church in the world.

Then the text seeks to describe those modes that are proper to both Scripture and Tradition and those that are different, insofar as these are manifestations, channels of the unique revelation of the Word of God. Scripture, first of all, is the act of God speaking (*locutio Dei*), insofar as it is recorded in writing under the breath of the Holy Spirit. Scripture is the written record, a record inspired by the Holy Spirit of God's own speaking. Scripture therefore contains the Word of God in written form, but the Word of God was first a living act whose recording was later inspired by the Holy Spirit. Here we see how Scripture flows from the one divine source which is revelation. First, there is the act of God who speaks, then the inspiration of the Holy Spirit who directs the act of writing, finally Scripture itself which is the record of the living Word of God. Tradition relays integrally the Word of God (*verbum Dei integre transmittit*) which was entrusted to the apostles

by Christ the Lord and by the Holy Spirit. It is clear that here
Tradition is understood essentially as the act of the faithful
relaying the Word of God. Tradition is not the Word of God
in the same sense as when it was said earlier that Scripture is
the act of God speaking recorded under the inspiration of the
Spirit. Tradition carries the Word of God just as it was entrusted to the apostles by Christ and the Spirit and relays it
integrally. So we see how Tradition flows from the one divine source, revelation. There is first the Word of God, then
the mandate of Christ and of the Spirit to the apostles who
decide what should be relayed, then Tradition itself, which is
the integral transmission of God's living Word.

If a comparison is made in this description between Scripture and Tradition, it will be noted that Scripture is the act of
the recorded Word of God and that Tradition *transmits integrally* the Word of God entrusted to the apostles. Scripture
is therefore to be distinguished from the Word of God or from
revelation only by the passage of the spoken word to the written word, and this passage is inspired by the Holy Spirit. Tradition is distinguished from the Word of God, or from revelation, in that it transmits the Word of God, which is none
other than itself, although carried on and linked to it by the
integrity of its transmission. Scripture is, and Tradition transmits integrally, the Word of God entrusted to the apostles by
Christ and the Spirit.

The text does not juxtapose Tradition to Scripture in trying
to define its proper constituents, but refers it to the single
source of the spoken Word of God which it carries and transmits integrally. This integral transmission of the spoken Word
of God is made to the successors of the apostles "so that, following the light of the Spirit of truth, these may faithfully
preserve, expound and spread it in their discourses."

Here an important distinction should be noted. The sentence about Tradition distinguishes between the spoken
Word of God entrusted to the apostles by Christ and the Spirit,
that is to say by inspiration and the ministry of the Word of

God exercised by the successors of the apostles in the light of the Spirit of truth (*praelucente Spiritu veritatis*), that is, with the assistance of the Holy Spirit. The Word of God transmitted by Tradition is a fruit of the *inspiration* of the Holy Spirit; the ministry of the Word of God, exercised by the successors of the apostles is a fruit of the *assistance* of the Holy Spirit. In the first case, the work of the apostles constitutes apostolic Tradition through the mandate of Christ and the inspiration of the Spirit. In the second case, the preaching of the successors is a service of the spoken Word of God which they received from Tradition, which they faithfully guard, develop, and make known with the assistance of the Spirit of truth; they can add nothing objectively to the content of apostolic Tradition, to the spoken Word of God given once and for all.

Here an important addition was made to the text before the vote on the *modi* (the last opportunity for modification): "Consequently, the Church does not draw her certainty about all that is revealed with the help of Holy Scripture alone." Cardinal Florit, Archbishop of Florence, explained in his intervention that this addition introduced no change in the substance of the schema but that it perfected its expression. The two most important justifications given in the intervention for this addition may be summed up in this way:

(1) Catholic doctrine, sanctioned by the constant practice of the Church, affirms that the Church draws its certitude about revealed truths from Sacred Scripture always united with Tradition; thus, when Scripture alone does not suffice to assure this certitude, Tradition can provide a decisive argument.

(2) The meaning of this statement should be judged and circumscribed according to the tenor of the schema, according to which (a) Tradition is not presented as a quantitative *supplement* of Sacred Scripture, (b) Sacred Scripture is not presented as a *codification* of integral revelation.

First of all, the importance of the word "certitude" should be stressed. In this addition there is no question of the objective existence of revealed realities which would not be found absolutely in Scripture and which should be looked for in Tradition. It is Tradition's role to affirm the certitude of the Church on the subject of certain revealed matters for which Scripture alone cannot provide complete certitude; this is not to say that Scripture does not in any way contain all these revealed truths, even implicitly, and that they can be found only in Tradition. *Sola Traditio* is no more true than *sola Scriptura* for certain special truths. The Church draws its certitude, in regard to revelation, from Scripture always conjoined to Tradition, and when Scripture does not suffice to establish certitude, Tradition does not supply the objective reality of a truth that might be missing in Scripture but a decisive argument for the certitude of the Church concerning this truth which is not stated explicitly in Scripture alone.

Tradition, therefore, is not a quantitative supplement to Scripture; there are no truths of Tradition which should be added to those of Scripture; they each carry the same revelation. Nevertheless, Scripture is not a codification of integral revelation. The Bible is not a code that has been dropped from heaven and whose affirmations are immediately self-evident. Because Scripture is itself the fruit of a living apostolic Tradition, it needs for its deciphering the heart of the apostolic Church. To say that Scripture is the Word of God recorded under the inspiration of the Holy Spirit does not mean that it can be in all its parts immediately understood in the fullness of its meaning and in all its implications. Because it is the fruit of the living Tradition of the Church, Scripture needs to be read and interpreted in the life of the Church, in conjunction with Tradition to be fully understood in all its significance and implications. If Scripture is recognized as God's living Word, it cannot be isolated (*sola Scriptura*) from the life of the Church and from Tradition.

This statement can be verified by a study of certain truths of the Christian faith as, for example, trinitarian and christological dogmas. It cannot be denied that God manifests himself in Scripture, that he speaks and acts there as the one God, as Father, Son and Spirit. Yet the trinitarian dogma of our Christian faith comes to us as the summary guaranteed and confirmed by Tradition of this trinitarian truth present in the history of salvation, and reported by Scripture. Nor can there be any doubt that in the Gospel, Christ appears as the Son of God and as a man; yet the christological dogma of the two natures is an authentic explanation of Tradition which guarantees our faith in Christ, true God and true man, as he appears in Scripture. For other truths in Scripture which are more implicit and which Scripture alone would not enable us to discover with certitude, the living Tradition of the Church provides a decisive argument. This is undoubtedly true of the dogma of Christ's real presence in the eucharist. This real presence, which has been part of the Church's liturgical life since apostolic days, throws a decisive light on the interpretation of some short New Testament texts describing the institution by Christ at the Last Supper. Here, the living Tradition concerning the eucharist provides a decisive argument for our certitude about the real presence which is implicitly attested to by Scripture in its eucharistic texts.

This whole development recalls the Montreal text already quoted: "The Scriptures as documents can be letter only. It is the Spirit who is the Lord and giver of life. Accordingly we may say that the right interpretation (taking the words in the widest possible sense) is that interpretation which is guided by the Holy Spirit." [5]

For the Council, the Holy Spirit is the soul of the living Tradition of the Church, and this Tradition is not to be separated from Scripture so that the Church may reach plenary certitude about all revealed truths.

No Christian confession escapes this union of Tradition and Scripture. In fact, every Christian approaches Scripture with a formation inherited from the tradition in which he was born. Each Church supports the certitude of its teaching through

[5] *Ibid.*, Sec. II, no. 52.

Scripture interpreted in the light of her tradition. Which Church could claim to interpret Scripture by itself without introducing the argument of tradition in its interpretation? Which one could insist that its belief rests solely on the basis of Scripture? The Montreal Conference noted with some humor: "We are more aware of the fact that we live according to different confessional traditions and this is paradoxically expressed in this way: It is the tradition of my Church not to attach any weight to tradition!" To refer again to the example of eucharistic faith, there is no doubt that different Christian confessions which have often taken opposite sides on the question of the real presence introduce into their interpretation of these Scripture texts on the eucharist arguments derived not only from objective exegesis but also from ecclesial tradition, theological systems, and liturgical experience.

We now come to the problem of criteria, the hermeneutical principle: "The necessity of interpretation raises again the question of the criterion for the genuine Tradition . . . This problem has been dealt with in different ways by the various Churches. In some confessional traditions the accepted hermeneutical principle has been that any portion of Scripture is to be interpreted in the light of Scripture as a whole. In others the key had been sought in what is considered to be the center of Holy Scripture, and the emphasis has been primarily on the incarnation, or on the atonement and redemption, or on justification by faith, or again on the message of the nearness of the Kingdom of God, or on the ethical teachings of Jesus. In yet others, all emphasis is laid upon what Scripture says to the individual conscience, under the guidance of the Holy Spirit. In the Orthodox Church the hermeneutical key is found in the mind of the Church, especially as expressed in the Fathers of the Church and in the Ecumenical Councils. In the Roman Catholic Church the key is found in the deposit of faith, of which the Church's *magisterium* is the guardian. In other traditions again the creeds, complemented by confessional documents or by the definitions of Ecumenical Coun-

cils and the witness of the Fathers, are considered to give the
right key to the understanding of Scripture. In none of these
cases where the principle of interpretation is found elsewhere
than in Scripture is the authority thought to be alien to the
central concept of Holy Scripture. On the contrary, it is considered as providing just a key to the understanding of what
is said in Scripture." [6]

Once again we see how in Montreal the problems raised are
similar to those of Vatican II. Yet the major and decisive is-
sue remains the question of the criterion of the true Tradition
and the correct interpretation of Scripture. Here Montreal is
satisfied to give the Churches' different answers. Later we will
see the answer of Vatican II.

This doctrinally important paragraph closes with an exhortation to receive and venerate Scripture and Tradition with
the same love and respect.

As a conclusion to our reflections on this paragraph concerning the relations between Scripture and Tradition let us give
a quotation from a recent manual of theology (P. Grelot,
Bible et Théologie) which seems to us to summarize Catholic
thought along conciliar lines. First he proposes a thesis: "In
order to preserve correctly and integrally the Gospel of Christ,
ecclesiastical tradition finds in Scripture the criterion for its
own faith; but in return it expresses the rule for its interpretation in different ways." [7] Then the author develops his
thought in these words: "Until the Middle Ages, theologians
admitted the principle of the sufficiency of Scripture for the
establishment of the foundations of faith. Not that it is possible to draw from Scripture alone all the dogmatic truths to
be accepted; but because Scripture when read according to
Tradition gives the roots of these truths under one form or
another. It is true that nothing can be affirmed against its
formal testimony and everything can be presented as coming
from it. It is to this that theology and preaching should tend

[6] *Ibid.*, Sec. II, 51, 53.
[7] P. Grelot, *Bible et Théologie*, p. 92.

because it is the proper role of theology to place us in direct contact with apostolic sources. Once the organic relations of Scripture and ecclesiastical tradition are stated in these words, it becomes clear that the essential problem confronting theologians is hermeneutics, that is to say, the interpretation of Scripture because their whole purpose is to bring together, beginning with occasional and limited texts, the totality of the apostolic legacy without losing anything of its original richness." [8]

10. Relation of Both with the Church and the Magisterium

Tradition and Scripture form a single deposit of the Word of God, which is entrusted to the Church. The Constitution once again insists on the unity of Scripture and Tradition which together carry on the Word of God, each in its own way; one transmits this Word integrally, the other is this Word recorded in writing. The Word of God is the source of both; it is contained and transmitted by both; it constitutes their profound unity.

By adhering to this unique deposit of the word of God entrusted to the Church, the faithful, together with their pastors, are able to reproduce the life of the apostolic Church and to persevere in the doctrine of the apostles and fraternal communion, in the breaking of bread and in prayer (cf. Acts 2, 42, Greek text). Thus, in the preservation, the practice, and the confession of traditional faith, the unity of spiritual leaders and faithful is realized.

The Council then faces the problem of the criterion of the authentic interpretation of the Word of God written or transmitted, that is, the problem of the authorized minister of this interpretation. This charge, this ministry of the authentic interpretation of Scripture and Tradition, was entrusted only

[8] *Ibid.*, pp. 95-96.

to the Church's living magisterium whose authority is exercised in the name of Jesus Christ; that is, according to the ec-
clesiological vocabulary of Vatican II, to the bishops, teaching
in communion with the Roman Pontiff, who must be respected by all as witnesses of the divine and catholic truth:
"But when either the Roman Pontiff or the body of bishops
together with him defines a judgment, they pronounce it in
accord with revelation itself. All are obliged to maintain and
be ruled by this revelation, which, as written or preserved by
tradition, is transmitted in its entirety through the legitimate
succession of bishops and especially through the care of the
Roman Pontiff himself.

"[Revelation] under the guiding light of the Spirit of truth
is religiously preserved and faithfully expounded in the
Church. The Roman Pontiff and the bishops, in view of their
office and the importance of the matter, by fitting means dili-
gently strive to inquire properly into that revelation and to
give apt expression to its contents; but they do not accept a
new public revelation as pertaining to the divine deposit of
faith." [9]

Here is the Roman Catholic solution to the question of
criterion and authority in regard to the interpretation of Scripture and the discernment of authentic Tradition, a question
discussed at Montreal and one whose solution divides Christians. In general, Protestantism sees in the Catholic solution
of the magisterium, which is authorized to give an authentic
interpretation, the danger that it will eventually be placed
above Scripture and cannot itself be judged by the Word of
God, the supreme norm of faith and doctrine. Although Vatican II did not present on this point an answer that Protestantism can accept as perfectly satisfactory, it is worth noting
as an ecumenical sign, that the Constitution on revelation
now tries to indicate the relation between the magisterium
and the Word of God in a new way.

First, there is the clear statement that the magisterium is

[9] *The Constitution on the Church,* chap. 3, no. 25.

not above the Word of God (*Magisterium non supra verbum Dei est*). The magisterium is at the service of the Word; it teaches only what has been transmitted. It has received a mission from God to perform this task, and the Holy Spirit assists it in this ministry. It listens with love to this Word of God to keep it reverently and to expound it faithfully. Whatever it proposes to the believing Church as part of divine revelation, it draws from the unique deposit of faith, which is the Word of God recorded in Scripture and transmitted by Tradition. The responsibility which rests on the magisterium—the pope and the bishops—to teach in service to the Word, is a heavy one. The insistence of the Constitution on the conception of the doctrinal ministry as a service should be noted. It is indeed characteristic of Vatican II to insist on the service that should be linked with authority in the Church, just as much as on the power it enjoys through God's mandate and the assistance of the Holy Spirit. No one can deny that it enjoys this power, but it is to serve the Word of God and the Church, not to dominate them.

The magisterium, as a service of the Word of God, is charged to teach nothing but this transmitted Word; it is also charged to listen respectfully and lovingly, to preserve it conscientiously and expound it exactly; and it is finally charged to draw from the one deposit of faith, the written and transmitted Word of God, everything that is proposed for belief as divinely revealed.

The service of the Word of God is a heavy responsibility, but to accomplish this it enjoys the mandate of God and the assistance of the Holy Spirit. The insistence on the magisterium's service does not diminish the certitude of its authority mandated and assisted by the Lord of the Church. This, again, is something that divides Christians. Even though traditional Protestantism also believes in a ministry that is divine in origin and is aided by the Holy Spirit for the service of the Word of God, this ministry is regarded as an instrument which God uses but which, because of its human condition, searches, may be deceived, and does not enjoy infallibility which is the possession of the Word of God which it serves.

Protestantism always tries to keep the independence of the Word of God in relation to the ministry of the Church and in this way makes it possible for the Word of God to judge the ministry of the Church. The conciliar text plainly and fully affirms the fidelity of the magisterium towards the Word of God which it serves, at least at those moments when the infallibility of the Church or of the pope is made manifest, and a truth is proposed for belief as divinely revealed. The problem of the infallibility of the Church remains a problem which ought to be studied in ecumenical dialogue. But once again it is of great ecumenical import that the Council insisted that the magisterium of the Church is at the service of the Word of God which is clearly stated to be in no way beneath the Word of God which it serves.

Chapter II closes with a sentence full of doctrinal and ecumenical meaning. This is the clear statement of the indissoluble link between Tradition, Scripture, and the magisterium. All three are so bound together and interrelated that one cannot stand without the other (*ut unum sine aliis non consistat*). Without Scripture, Tradition cannot know its true apostolic content, because it would have no reference to the apostolic Tradition recorded in Scripture; without the magisterium, Tradition cannot be certain that it is truly the Tradition of the Church that begins with the apostles because it has no authentic interpreter to discern between the faithful transmission of the Word of God and traditions that are purely ecclesiastical. Without Tradition, Scripture runs the risk of being no more than testimony of the past, without any true life in the Church or to be delivered to individual interpretation without reference to the universal and continued interpretation of the Word of God; without the magisterium, Scripture is not read and understood in the Church and loses its authority in the dispersion of contradictory interpretations. Without Tradition, the magisterium is a passing authority which assures no continuity of faith in the Church; without Scripture, the magisterium has no objective reference to apostolic Tradition which enables it to discern what conforms to the Word of God and what does not.

It follows that Tradition, Scripture, and the magisterium should advance together. Each expresses the Word of God in its own way: Tradition through living transmission in the Church, Scripture through written recording in the Bible, the magisterium through authoritative interpretation in the Church. These different expressions of the Word of God are all directed by the same Holy Spirit: Scripture by inspiration (*sub inspiratione Spiritus Sancti*), Tradition and the magisterium by the help and light of the Spirit (*Spiritu Sancto assistente, praelucenta Spiritu veritatis*). These three modes of the expression of the one Word of God together contribute effectively to the salvation of men. Thus, according to this text, the magisterium—pope and bishops—can offer for belief as a truth that has been divinely revealed only the Word of God contained in Scripture and transmitted by Tradition.

This statement is rich in ecumenical consequences. But it is plain that between separated Christians there arises the problem of the authentic ministry and its exercise in interpreting the deposit of faith, Scripture and Tradition. A big step has been taken: there is a better understanding of the relation between Scripture and Tradition. Another step is now of importance in ecumenical dialogue: the understanding of what the magisterium is in the Church, the ministry of the authentic interpretation of Scripture and Tradition, by way of proposing divinely revealed truth for belief.

III
HOLY SCRIPTURE:
DIVINE INSPIRATION
AND INTERPRETATION

11. The Inspiration of the Truth of Holy Scripture Established as a Fact

This paragraph begins with a categorical statement about the inspiration of Scripture. The revelation which is contained in Scripture is presented in written form; this writing was done under the influx of the Holy Spirit (*Spiritu Sancto afflante*). The Church, founded on the faith of the apostles, considers as sacred and canonical all the books of the Old and New Testament, in all their parts because as they were written under the inspiration of the Holy Spirit (*Spiritu Sancto inspirante*), it is God himself who is their author and as such they have been transmitted to the Church. Here the Constitution cites several Scripture texts affirming the divine inspiration of the Bible. After John 20, 31, comes the text of 2 Tim. 3, 16: "Every Scripture is divinely inspired and useful: it educates, it argues, it corrects, it teaches discipline, that the man of God may be perfect and instructed in every good deed." Reference is also made to 2 Pet. 1, 19-21 and 3, 15-16: "And we have the word of prophecy, surer still, to which you do well to attend, as to a lamp shining in a dark place, until the day dawns and the morning star arises in your hearts. This, then, you must understand first of all, that no prophecy of Scripture is made by private interpretation. For not by will of man was prophecy brought at any time; but holy men of

54

God spoke as they were moved by the Holy Spirit . . . And regard the long-suffering of our Lord as salvation. Just as our most dear brother Paul also, according to the wisdom given him, has written to you, as indeed he did in all his epistles, speaking in them of these things. In these epistles there are certain things difficult to understand, which the unlearned and the unstable distort, just as they do the rest of the Scriptures also, to their own destruction." This last quotation shows that the author of 2 Peter accepted Paul's letters as part of inspired and canonical Scripture.

The text goes on to show how the Council looks at the relation between God, the author of Sacred Scripture, and the sacred writers who are the inspired authors of the different books of the Bible. For the composition of these holy books, God chose men whom he employed, acting himself in them and through them so that they might transmit all that he wished. But these men, chosen and employed by God, acted always as men: they used their limited, human faculties and power to record, as truly personal authors, what they were to transmit under the inspiration of the Spirit and according to the will of God. It was the Holy Spirit acting in and through these men who united without confounding, God, who is the author of the written revelation and the human authors of Scripture. Thus, these human authors could in spite of their limited faculties and power transmit as revealed all that God wished and only what he wished. This very firm doctrine of the inspiration of Scripture asserts both the divine character of written revelation, which has God for its author, and the human character of Scripture, which has men for its authors. This means that the inspired character of the Bible need in no way be diminished, and at the same time it justifies the use of scientific methods of exegesis in the study of texts. Holy Scripture can be studied as an aggregate of texts composed by human authors using their own faculties and powers, but it cannot be studied from that point of view alone, for these men were inspired by the Holy Spirit who acted in and through them so that they could accomplish God's will when they wrote; that is, so that they could transmit everything that he wanted and only what he wanted revealed, and so that the writings of which they were the true authors would also have God for their author.

Thus, all that these inspired authors affirm is also to be considered as affirmed by the Holy Spirit. Scripture therefore teaches firmly, faithfully, and faultlessly the truth that God wished there to be put down for our salvation. Scripture, of which God is the author, does not contain merely any kind of truth, but truth that has been revealed for our salvation and that, also for our salvation, God wished to be put down in the Bible. Here the Constitution cites several authorities including the Council of Trent which says apropos of the Gospel that it is "the source of all salutary truth and of the whole moral code" (Sess. IV, Decr. *De Canonicis Scripturis*). Vatican II did not use the expression "salutary truth," which today might suggest to some a limited extension of inerrancy. They might think that only those parts of Scripture dealing directly with salvation were surely free from error. On this point there could be a wide variety of opinions, some more restrictive than others. The Council preferred to say that inerrancy concerns the truth that God consigned to Scripture for the sake of our salvation. This truth cannot be restricted to a few elements and as a whole concerns our salvation. It is for our salvation that God consigned it to Scripture. This is to use the Council of Trent's expression "salutary truth" in its widest and most inclusive sense: Scripture teaches revealed truth firmly, faithfully, and faultlessly, and this truth which concerns our salvation has been consigned by God for our salvation. A statement as strong as this shows clearly that Scripture contains all the revealed truth necessary for salvation. In this can be seen another sign that the doctrine of the Council is moving toward the idea that the whole of revelation is contained in some way in Scripture, that Tradition therefore can add nothing to it quantitatively, even though it is a necessary aid for explaining and explicitating this revelation contained in Scripture, and that Tradition faithfully continues in the Church.

This fullness of Scripture as revelation is also emphasized in the biblical citation that closes this paragraph: "Every Scripture is divinely inspired and useful: it educates, it argues, it corrects, it teaches discipline, that the man of God may be perfect and instructed in every good deed" (2 Tim. 3, 16-17). If through Scripture the man of God is perfect (*artios*), instructed (*exertismenos*) in every good deed, it is because Scripture provides him with all the elements needed for this perfecting and instructing. The Latin of the Vulgate, ". . . *ut perfectus sit homo Dei, ad omne opus bonum instructus* . . ." is translated as ". . . so that the man of God can be perfect and formed for every good work." The revelation that is contained in the inspired Scripture can make the man of God perfect; Scripture therefore contains all the truth that is necessary for this perfection. The Tradition living in the Church adds nothing to this; it can explain and explicitate it because it carries and transmits this same truth under a different form.

12. How Holy Scripture Is To Be Interpreted

The interpretation of Holy Scripture is commanded by the double fact that it is God who spoke in it and he has spoken through men and in the way that men speak. The understanding of what God wished to reveal therefore necessarily implies the search for the true intention of the human inspired authors and for God's intention through their words.

Therefore, the methods of scientific exegesis must be applied to these human writings that bring us the very Word of God. The text examines the problem of literary forms. There are in Scripture different levels of historical texts: There are prophetic texts, poetic texts, and many others. The different authors of Scripture found themselves in different situations according to their circumstances, epoch, or culture, and different literary forms were in vogue at different times. It follows that the interpreter of Scripture should try to discover what the author wanted to say and what he actually said. To grasp the author's purpose, attention should be paid to the ways of feeling, speaking, and relating that were his heritage at that moment and to the usual forms of communication then in use among men. Here the Council refers to the encyclical *Divino afflante Spiritu* of September 30, 1943, of Pius XII, where problems of exegesis are treated at length.

But if Scripture, as with everything else written by man, should be interpreted according to the methods of historical science, it should also be read and interpreted according to the Holy Spirit who is its author. It would be unscientific for the Church to study Scripture as if it were no more than a human document governed only by the laws of historical science. As a matter of fact, Scripture is the fruit of a mystery of the union between God, its author, and men, its inspired authors. If, then, true science is to be applied to the interpretation of Scripture, it should be read in the same spirit in which it was written, and this spirit is the Holy Spirit who has inspired and guided the authors of the sacred texts. To place ourselves in the school of the Holy Spirit in the scientific exegesis of Scripture means that we should attentively consider Scripture as a whole and not only its isolated texts. There is indeed a divine intention in revelation that marks the whole content of the Bible and which gives it a fundamental unity. The living Tradition of the whole Church guided by the Holy Spirit discovers this unity of Scripture in the Holy Spirit who inspired it and affirms the principle of the analogy of faith. According to this analogy of faith, God does not contradict himself in revelation, and one aspect of revealed truth should be situated in the general context of the whole history of God's revelation to men, recorded in the whole of Scripture which is one in its historical and literary diversity.

When exegetes apply these rules, they are able to deepen and explain the meaning of Scripture and through their study, which is preparatory, they mature the judgment of the Church. It is of the utmost importance that the judgment of the Church be enlightened and develop because she is the ultimate judge of everything that concerns the interpretation of Scripture. She has received from God the mandate and ministry of preserving and interpreting the Word of God. The close connection between exegetes responsible for the maturing of the judgment of the Church and the magisterium responsible for guarding and interpreting the Word of God will make sure that there is neither a failure in understanding nor a rupture between exegetical science applied to Scripture and ecclesiastical authority responsible for the revealed deposit.

13. God's Condescendence

This paragraph discusses the humanity of Scripture as a sign of God's "condescension" for man. It adopts the idea of St. John Chrysostom (cf. Gen. 3, 8) where we find the Greek term *synkatábasis* which means that God descends to our human level to be with us in his revelation and thus to make it available to us. The word "condescension" has the same etymological meaning, but we must free it from all the pejorative nuances that it has in English. Pius XII also quoted St. John Chrysostom in his encyclical *Divino afflante Spiritu.*

In the humanity of Scripture is manifested the "condescension" of God's eternal wisdom, who is willing in order to reveal himself to men to place himself wholly at their disposition, in a language which they can understand, while allowing nothing to affect the truth and holiness of revelation. Scripture, in its humanity, becomes therefore a sign of God's goodness and of the care he takes of our nature to adapt himself to it while revealing his truth and holiness.

The chapter closes with a comparison between God's "condescension" in Scripture and the incarnation of the Word of God in human flesh. In Scripture the Word of God is expressed in a human language; the divine Word becomes similar (*assimile*) to the human word just as once Jesus Christ, the Word of God, took our human flesh and became similar (*simile*) to men. Obviously, this is only a comparison showing that God's condescension in Scripture matches that in the incarnation. There is no question of another form of incarnation of the Word of God in the human language of Scripture. The Word of God is expressed (*verba expressa*) in a human language, and there is indeed a close union of the two; while in the incarnation of Jesus Christ the Word took our human flesh (*assumpta carne*). The distinction is also indicated when the text says that the words of God in Scripture have become "like to" (*assimilia*) the human word, while the Word of God in the incarnation has become "like" (*simile*) men. This comparison gives a deep spiritual value to the humanity of Scripture. It is not in spite of this humanity but through it that the Word of God in all truth and holiness comes to man, on his own level and in his own language. This makes clear that God is really with us in written revelation according to the ineffable benevolence which in times past brought him in our midst so that he might dwell among us in Jesus Christ.

IV
THE OLD COVENANT

14. The History of Salvation Consigned to the Books of the Old Covenant

This chapter on the Old Testament traces the broad outlines of the theological thought of the first part of the Bible.

For the salvation of all men and to prepare for this salvation, God chose in a special way the Jewish people in order to entrust his promises to them. First, he made a covenant with Abraham, then with Moses for the people of Israel. He revealed himself to them in words and in deeds. Once again, the text insists on the fact that the revelation is communicated not only by words expressing truths, but also by acts which make concrete God's truth and love. Thus, God revealed himself to Israel as the one, true, and living God; there is only one God and he is a personal God. This is the personalist monotheism which was to become the fundamental doctrine of the Jewish people.

Furthermore, revelation made it possible for Israel to live the experience of the life of God among men, to enter into an ever deeper understanding of this life and to give witness to it among all people. God, unique and personal, is present to his People, and speaks to them through the mouths of his prophets. Jewish personalist monotheism is therefore at the same time opposed to polytheism, pantheism, and deism, affirming as it does that there is only one, true, personal God who is present through his Word.

The history of salvation, lived by the chosen People, is

proclaimed, related and explained by the authors of the Old
Covenant. This constitutes the very Word of God to his people as revealed by words and acts. Thus, the inspired texts
have a value for all time. St. Paul states this in the Epistle to
the Romans (15, 4): "Whatever was written, was written for
our instruction, that, through perseverance and with the help
of the Scriptures, we may have hope." The Scripture of the
Old Covenant gives us constancy and consolation and justifies
our hope. To read the history of the chosen People is to learn
patience in God's school of patience, to experience the riches
of the consolation that he knew how to bestow on his faithful
witnesses, to understand the meaning of hope, to see the People of God who, despite persecution, never ceased to look forward to the coming of the Messiah-Savior.

15. The Importance of the Old Covenant for Christians

Here the Old Covenant is considered as the preparation for
the coming of Christ, the universal Savior, and his messianic
Kingdom. The Old Covenant contains prophetic proclama-
tions and significant figures. It witnesses to knowledge of God
and man, to God's ways of dealing with men according to his
justice and mercy. Evidently this knowledge and this pedagogy
are adapted to pre-Christian times and to the human condition in its evolution until the coming of Christ. The Old
Testament therefore contains imperfect and temporary elements, but it demonstrates God's pedagogy, preparing men to
welcome Christ as Messiah and Savior.

Because of the revelation of divine pedagogy that the books
of the Old Covenant contain, Christians should receive them
with reverence. They reveal an understanding of God who is
unique, personal, and present in his Word; they reveal a
wisdom of human life which leads to salvation and treasures
of prayer. The whole divine work of man's salvation is hidden
in the Old Testament to be clearly manifested in the New.

16. The Unity of the Two Covenants

God himself is the inspirer and author of the two Testaments. In his wisdom he arranged that the New would be mysteriously present in the Old and that in the New would be found the development of the Old: *"Ut Novum in Vetere lateret et in Novo Vetus pateret,"* according to St. Augustine's thought.[1] The New Testament, founded in the blood of Christ, did not put an end to the use of the Old Testament. In fact, the books of the Old Testament are recognized in the New as inspired and canonical. They form part of the evangelical preaching, and the apostles cite them in their inspired writings. In the New Testament, the texts of the Old receive their full significance which was hidden until the coming of Christ. On the other hand, the Old Testament enables us to grasp the full meaning of the New, recalling its origin and preparation, its cultural and religious setting, and the fact that it is the fulfillment of the history of salvation which was begun in the Old Covenant. It continues without interruption or discontinuity in the New.

[1] *Quaest. in Hept.* 2, 73.

V
THE NEW COVENANT

17. The Excellence of the New Covenant

It is clear that the Word of God is present in the New Testament in a unique way and in all its power, a divine power for the salvation of every believer (cf. Rom. 1, 16). The text of this paragraph summarizes in broad outline the content of the New Testament: the incarnation of the Word, the establishment of the reign of God by Christ, the manifestation in acts and words of the Father and the Son, the death, resurrection, and ascension of the Lord, the sending of the Holy Spirit, and the action of the glorious Christ on all men. This whole mystery of Christ was revealed to the apostles and prophets of the New Covenant through the inspiration of the Holy Spirit so that they might preach it as the Good News, call all men to the faith, and assemble them in the Church. The New Testament is the permanent and inspired testimony of the mystery of Christ, received and proclaimed by the apostles.

18. The Apostolic Origin of the Gospels

In all Scripture and in the New Testament itself, the four Gospels have a special place because they contain the life and teaching of Christ, the Word made flesh. The Council affirms that always and everywhere the Church has recognized the apostolic origin of the four Gospels. In fact the Gospel under its four forms recalls the preaching of the apostles according to the mission received from Christ; the apostles themselves, as well as the apostolic men, the evangelists, transmitted this preaching to us in writing under the inspiration of the Holy Spirit. This Gospel in its fourfold form is the foundation of Christian faith.

19. The Historic Character of the Gospels

The Council clearly affirms the historicity of the Gospels. They faithfully transmit what Christ really did and taught for the eternal salvation of men during his life until his ascension. After his ascension the apostles transmitted his words and his acts with the deepened insight resulting from his glorious events (the resurrection, the apparitions, the ascension) and from the light of the Holy Spirit who had introduced them since Pentecost into the whole truth. Therefore, the Gospels are not a historic report about Jesus as in the case of men; they are a testimony reporting the historic words and deeds of the Son of God made man which are understood in depth, thanks to the light of the risen Christ and the inspiration of the Holy Spirit.

The composition of the Gospels is the result of a choice made among many oral and written testimonies; the inspired authors sometimes summarized the events of Christ's life or his discourses; sometimes they offered an explanation so that his deeds and words could be better understood by the Churches at a particular moment. Lastly, they gave their writings a kerygmatic form which corresponded to their sources, which were certainly narratives preached at liturgical gatherings or adapted to the catechesis. Nevertheless, these choices, these summaries, these explanations, these styles detract in no way from the fundamentally historic character of the Gospels. The constant intention of the inspired authors is to communicate and to transmit sincerely and truthfully what was known about Jesus.

Taking their own remembrances or what they could recall, or using the accounts of eyewitnesses and of the earliest
preachers, they set down with the firm intention of sharing
with us the solid truth of the testimonies which they faithfully transmitted, and which constitute the teaching that the
Christians received as the basis of their faith (cf. Luke 1, 2-4).
On the basis of their own remembrances and what they were
able to recall or using the words of the eyewitnesses and first
preachers, all this preparatory work of the evangelists, apostles, or apostolic men was sustained and guided by the Holy
Spirit, who inspired them and led them in perfect truth.
Thus, the four Gospels, as the other Scriptures, are at the same
time a human work that is serious and honest, and a divine
work accomplished by the Holy Spirit, who inspired and directed the evangelists.

Christ promised the apostles: "But when he, the Spirit of
truth, has come, he will teach you all the truth. For he will not
speak on his own authority, but whatever he will hear he will
speak, and the things that are to come he will declare to you.
He will glorify me, because he will receive of what is mine and
declare it to you. All things that the Father has are mine. That
is why I have said that he will receive of what is mine, and will
declare it to you" (John 16, 13-15). This text underlines the
unity of revelation: it has its source in God the Father; it was
proclaimed by the Son; it was inspired by the Holy Spirit, who
reminded and taught the evangelists what Christ had said:
"But the Advocate, the Holy Spirit, whom the Father will
send in my name, he will teach you all things, and bring to
your mind whatever I have said to you" (John 14, 26).

20. The Other Writings of the New Covenant

The other writings of the New Covenant are the fruit of the
same inspiration of the Holy Spirit. They confirm all that concerns Christ, illumine the depths of his authentic teaching,

and proclaim the power of his redemptive work (the epistles). They relate the beginnings and expansion of the primitive Church (the Acts of the Apostles) and announce the glorious consummation of the Church (the Apocalypse).

This inspiration of the whole New Testament is based on the promise of Christ to be always with his apostles (cf. Matt. 28, 20), and to send them the Spirit of truth to lead them into the fullness of truth (cf. John 15, 13).

VI
HOLY SCRIPTURE
IN THE CHURCH'S LIFE

21. The Church Venerates Holy Scripture

The last chapter of the Constitution seems at first to be a spiritual and practical text in which consequences are drawn for the life of the Church from the other more doctrinal chapters. As a matter of fact, it is deeply doctrinal and even introduces fresh support for the new orientation that we have been emphasizing from the very beginning. It may be considered as a key to the understanding of the whole Constitution.

It opens with a very beautiful and traditional comparison between Scripture and the eucharist. The Church venerates Holy Scripture just as it venerates the eucharist. The Church venerates at the same time Holy Scripture and the body of the Lord, particularly in the liturgy. There is but one table from which the Church takes the bread of life to offer it to the faithful: the table of the Word of God and of the body of Christ (*mensa tam verbi Dei quam Corporis Christi*). This parallel between the two forms of the bread of life (Word and eucharist) balances doctrine and liturgy. There has been at times a tendency to exalt the sacrament to such a degree that the Word had only the minor role of explaining the essential event— Christ's eucharistic presence. Here, the affirmation that the table of the bread of life is that of the Word and of the sacrament better clarifies the position of the Word in the liturgical mystery: it is like the body of Christ, a presence, an act, food. Admittedly the eucharist remains a unique presence, act, and food, but to it the Word is indissolubly united to manifest Christ's work in his Church.

The consequences of this idea can be seen in the Constitution on the Liturgy where a very important place is given to the proclamation and preaching of the Word of God in the eucharistic celebration: "The treasures of the Bible are to be opened up more lavishly, so that richer fare may be provided for the faithful at the table of God's Word. In this way a more representative portion of the holy Scriptures will be read to the people in the course of a prescribed number of years. By means of the homily the mysteries of the faith and the guiding principles of the Christian life are expounded from the sacred text, during the course of the liturgical year; the homily, therefore, is to be highly esteemed as part of the liturgy itself; in fact, at those Masses which are celebrated with the assistance of the people on Sundays and feasts of obligation, it should not be omitted except for a serious reason." [1] The affirmation of the close union between Word and eucharist has considerable ecumenical importance.

Holy Scripture together with Holy Tradition is the supreme rule of the faith of the Church; in fact, they have been inspired by God and set in writing once and for all; they unfailingly communicate the Word of God himself and they contain the voice of the Holy Spirit in the words of the prophets and apostles. This sentence is most important for the understanding and interpretation of the whole Constitution on Revelation.

First of all, it throws new light on the relation between Scripture and Tradition. Scripture is the subject of the sentence: Scripture is the supreme rule of the faith of the Church. Of course, as we have already seen, it is not Scripture *alone,* in isolation, nor is it Scripture *and* Tradition placed side by side, one added to the other; it is Scripture *along with* Tradition *(una cum).* These three expressions describe three different ideas about the relation between Scripture and Tradi-

---

[1] *The Constitution on the Sacred Liturgy,* chap. 3, nos. 51-52.

tion. The sixteenth-century Reformation insisted on Scripture as the unique norm of faith, Scripture *alone;* this idea enhanced the importance of the Bible in the theology and life of the Church but it ran the risk of isolating Scripture from the Church and from its interpretation in Tradition; Scripture could become in its isolation open to excessively individualistic interpretations. The reaction of post-Tridentine theology was to insist on the role of Tradition beside Scripture to know the whole of revelation that is contained partly in one and partly in the other; granted that the Council of Trent did not say this expressly, the anti-Protestant reaction, nonetheless, tended toward this interpretation. This idea ran the risk of juxtaposing Scripture and Tradition on the same plane and of looking on the latter as a quantitative addition to the former. The great value of Vatican II is that it transcended these two ideas. Scripture *together with* Tradition is the supreme rule of the faith of the Church. This supreme rule is neither Scripture alone in isolation, nor Scripture and Tradition juxtaposed, but Scripture conjointly with Tradition, understood, interpreted, explicitated, confirmed by Tradition which faithfully transmits the Word of God in the Church.

This same method of transcendence may be found in several problems faced by Vatican II or in several positions of Catholicism today which have been influenced by the biblical, liturgical, and ecumenical renewal. This method of ecumenical transcendence might be symbolized by the phrase *una cum* (along with) which replaces the polemic or antithetical words *alone* (expressing exclusiveness) or *and* (expressing juxtaposition). In the following table we will show in relation to several theological points: (1) the exclusive and defensive method of the sixteenth-century Reform, (2) the method of juxtaposition and anti-Protestantism of post-Tridentine theology, (3) the inclusive and ecumenical method of transcendence in Catholicism renewed in the spirit of the Council:

(1) salvation by faith alone
(2) salvation by faith and works

(3) salvation by faith together with works expressed in charity.

(1) the unique sacrifice of the cross
(2) the sacrifice of the cross and the sacrifice of the Mass
(3) the sacrifice of the cross together with the Mass, sacramentalized, made present in the sacrificial memorial of the eucharist.

(1) the collegiate ministry
(2) the pope and the priesthood
(3) the pope together with the presbyterium. (Here may be cited the significant examples of the two forms of promulgation of conciliar texts in Vatican I and Vatican II. In Vatican I we read: "Pius, bishop, servant of the servants of God with the approbation of the Holy Council . . ." In Vatican II we read: "Paul, bishop, servant of the servants of God together with (*una cum*) the Fathers of the holy Council . . .")

(1) the universal and indivisible Church of the baptized elect
(2) the catholic, apostolic, and Roman Church and schismatics and heretics
(3) the Catholic Church together with, according to varying degrees of unity, the Churches or ecclesial communities not in communion with the pope.

(1) Scripture alone, source of revelation
(2) Scripture and Tradition, sources of revelation
(3) the Word of God, present in Scripture together with Tradition, source of revelation.

The spirit of the Second Vatican Council thus appears to be an attempt to transcend ecumenically and inclusively the exclusive positions of the past which could only maintain divisions among Christians. In this sense the Council is a first and decisive attempt of the Catholic Church to prepare itself for visible unity with other Christian communities.

So we see that the Council affirms that Scripture together with Tradition (understood, interpreted, explicitated, confirmed by Tradition which faithfully transmits the Word of God in the Church) is the supreme rule of faith in the Church. The unique position of faith is due to the fact that it alone has been inspired by God and once and for all consigned to writing. The Catholic Church never claimed that Tradition was inspired in the same way as Scripture; the living Tradition of the Church is assisted by the Holy Spirit to transmit faithfully the Word of God that it bears. As inspired by the Holy Spirit, Scripture enjoys a unique place in the Church: it is the supreme rule of faith together with Tradition which understands, interprets, explicitates and confirms it. On the other hand, Tradition progresses in the Church, it deepens and develops and the magisterium of the Church watches over this progress, this deepening, and development.

Scripture consigned in writing once and for all has a uniquely unchanging character. It is therefore the supreme and immutable rule of the faith of the Church; its inspiration and its immutability are a solid rock on which the Church rests. Furthermore, the text specifies that because of its inspiration and immutability Scripture communicates immutably the Word of God himself. In the reading and the proclamation of Scripture texts, the Church has the certitude that she is communicating the very Word of God. Finally the words of the prophets and of the apostles contained in Scripture bring to the Church the very voice of the Holy Spirit.

For these four reasons—inspiration by the Holy Spirit, immutable fixation in the texts and a canon, the unchanging Word of God that is communicated, the voice of the holy Spirit that rings out in the words of prophets and apostles— Scripture is the inspired, immutable, certain, and living rule, the supreme rule of faith on condition that it is read and understood in the living tradition of the Church. In fact, Scripture was not inspired and set down for its own sake or to remain an isolated code; it was inspired by God in the Church and for the Church which is a community of believers. But it was set down by God in the Church by means of inspired authors, and decisions concerning the canon, and for the Church, so that the Word of God himself might always be preserved immutably, and that in its words might always be heard the voice of the Holy Spirit.

Granted the unique position of Scripture, the supreme rule of faith, the Council declares that it should sustain and guide all preaching in the Church and the piety of Christians. On this point the text was changed and it is interesting to note its evolution in order to grasp the Council's purpose. In the schema amended for the third conciliar period of 1964, one may read: "All ecclesiastical preaching and Christian piety itself should always look to Scripture as to the norm and to the authority by which they are directed and judged." But because certain Fathers asked that Scripture be proposed less absolutely as the rule of all preaching, a new and much weaker amended text was suggested: "All ecclesiastical preaching like Christian piety itself should be nourished by Holy Scripture." At the time of the last correction in 1965, because a number of Fathers had asked that a return be made to a firmer formulation, it was suggested that a verb be added to the amended text of 1964: "that [all Church proclamation] must feed on, and be ruled by, Holy Scripture." This was accepted as the definitive text. The verb "judged" was omitted. These exchanges are typical of the Council's Theological Commission's desire for balance.

The actual text remains fairly strong in its affirmation that all preaching and religion (*religio*) should be nourished and guided by Scripture. Granted, the idea of the judgment of preaching and religion by Scripture has been suppressed. Yet in a most positive way, the text presents Scripture as the food of all preaching and religion; on the other hand, the idea of the norm and authority of Scripture is found in the verb *re-*

gere: Scripture directs, guides, governs, and rules the preaching of the Church and the religion of Christians. The ecumenical importance of the text can again be gauged.

Scripture is then described as the place where the Father comes lovingly to meet his children and to talk with them. This vision of the personal encounter of the Father with his children and of their friendly conversation recalls the parable of the prodigal son (cf. Luke 15, 20) and makes Scripture a lively place of encounter and dialogue where God's love for men is manifest. Scripture is not a code of laws, a book of history, a collection of sentences, or a manual of doctrines, but the living testimony of the love of God who meets men and converses with them. This living understanding of Scripture that the Council calls quite simply the Word of God makes it possible to recognize in it a power and dynamism which are the support and strength of the Church, the solidity of faith, the nourishment of the soul, the pure and never-failing source of the spiritual life of Christians. It seems as if the Council cannot find enough words to magnify the role of Scripture in the Church. A whole vocabulary of forceful and vital terms develops in this sentence: *vis, virtus, sustentaculum, vigor, robur, cibus, fons purus et perennis."* The paragraph closes with quotations from the New Testament applied to Sacred Scripture: The Word of God is living and efficacious. It is a power that constructs the edifice of the Church and that transmits the heritage of the Kingdom of God, which is the lot of all those who are sanctified (cf. Heb. 4, 12; Acts 20, 32).

22. Carefully Prepared Versions Are Recommended

The Council hopes for a wide distribution of the Bible, and this means translations in all the different modern languages. So that Christians could have easy access to Scripture, the ancient Church adopted the Greek version known as the Septuagint, then the Latin Vulgate as well as other oriental or

Latin versions. The Catholic Church still holds in high esteem these versions, especially the Vulgate, but wishes to have new versions in modern languages so that the Word of God will be present at all times. She recommends that these translations be based on original texts. It is interesting to note here that the Vulgate is considered above all as a modern translation of its time, made for wider distribution of the Bible and the actualization of the Word of God and that although the Catholic Church treats it with respect, she prefers translations based on original Hebrew or Greek texts.

The Council also considers positively translations which, with the approval of ecclesiastic authorities, might be made with non-Catholics and could consequently be used by all Christians speaking the same language. This is an ecumenical gesture of the Council which has already resulted in common translations being made in different places. The use of an identical text can contribute much to the unity of Christians in giving them a common tongue.

23. The Apostolic Task of Catholic Theologians

The paragraph is an exhortation and encouragement to exegetes and theologians so that they will continue with zeal their interpretation of Sacred Scripture. The Church is the Spouse of the incarnate Word; she is instructed by the Holy Spirit; she is therefore the servant of the Word of God. She seeks day by day to deepen her understanding of the Holy Scriptures so that she may nourish her children with the Word of God. In this work she is helped by the study of the Eastern and Western Fathers and by the liturgies. But she also expects much from modern exegetes and theologians who examine the Bible according to appropriate methods, and are guided by the magisterium. These biblical exegetes and theologians are at the service of pastors responsible for the nourishment of the People of God with the food of Scripture, which enlightens the mind, strengthens the will, kindles the heart. The paragraph closes with a powerfully encouraging word to theologians devoted to the study of the Bible so that they will bring their work to a happy conclusion by means of serious study according to the mind of the Church.

Here one is aware of the Council's pastoral preoccupation which rejoices over all modern exegetical work, but which fears that exegetes may become too independent; therefore, in their serious study of the Bible according to appropriate methods they are asked to recall the mind of the Church whose magisterium is charged with watching over the interpretation of Scripture and is responsible for the help given to pastors who are meant to distribute the nourishment of the Word of God to all the faithful.

24. The Importance of Holy Scripture for Theology

For the Council, theology is based on the written Word of God conjointly with Tradition as on a durable foundation; it is solidly strengthened and always kept young by the Word of God; it examines the whole truth hidden in the mystery of Christ. After some hesitations in the text, Tradition was situated in relation to Scripture as has been seen above: Tradition is not placed beside or added to Scripture but is conjoined to it (*una cum*). Scripture enlightened by Tradition is the foundation, the solidity, the youthfulness of theology whose task it is to penetrate the whole truth of the mystery of Christ in the light of faith. Here a very beautiful vision of theology is proposed, a theology deeply rooted in the written Word of God united with Tradition. The decree promulgated at the Council on priestly formation applies this vision in seminaries: "Students should receive a most careful training in Holy Scripture, which should be the soul, as it were, of all theology. After a suitable introductory course, they should receive an accurate initiation in exegetical method. They should study closely the principal themes of divine revelation and should find inspiration and nourishment in daily reading and meditation upon the sacred books. The following order should be observed in treatment of dogmatic theology: biblical themes should have first place." [2] It is easy to imagine the ecumenical fruits of a vision like this of Catholic theology and of such a program for the formation of future priests.

Then comes an important sentence, one of those key phrases that have been noted elsewhere: "The Holy Scriptures contain the Word of God and, on account of their inspiration, they are the Word of God. Accordingly, the study of the sacred text should be, so to speak, the soul of sacred theology." The Council does not hesitate to identify Scripture and the Word of God in virtue of the inspiration of the sacred texts. There is a progression in the sentence: Scripture *contains* the Word of God; Scripture that is inspired *is* the Word of God. Such an affirmation situates Scripture in a unique place in the Church. That is why the study of Scripture is, as it were, the soul of theology; we have already seen this affirmation in the Decree on Priestly Training; the Council holds to this formula. Of course, Tradition is united to Scripture, which it understands, interprets, explicitates, and confirms; but it is only of Scripture that one can say that it is inspired and therefore that it is truly the Word of God. So it is quite right to say that it is the soul of all theology.

The Word of Scripture should in the same way be made to nourish and strengthen the ministry of the Word: preaching, catechism, the whole work of Christian formation in which the liturgical homily is meant to play an important role. It is in Scripture that the ministry of the Word finds nourishment and health, strength and holiness (*salubriter nutritur sancteque virescit*). The Council insists on a strong statement that the whole life of the Church is based on Scripture, the Word of God, united with Tradition and that she draw thence all nourishment necessary for her health, her strength, and

[2] The Decree on Priestly Training, chap. 5, no. 16.

her holiness. Thus, the Catholic Church links her whole life with Holy Scripture, the Word of God.

25. The Reading of Holy Scripture Is Recommended

All the ministers of the Church are called to devote themselves to Scripture by careful reading and deep study so that they may listen to the Word of God before preaching and communicating all its infinite riches to the faithful, especially in the course of the liturgy.

The Council insistently exhorts all Christians and all religious to read Scripture frequently so that they may learn to know Jesus Christ. Following St. Jerome, the Council declares that: "Not to know Scripture is not to know Christ." To approach Scripture, there is liturgy which is full of the Word of God, there is personal reading of the Bible, there are courses in the Bible, etc. Prayer should be combined with the reading of Scripture so that there may be a true dialogue between God and man that means speaking to God in prayer and listening to him in reading, as St. Ambrose has said.

Bishops are responsible to train the faithful to use the Bible, especially the New Testament and above all the Gospels. They should make sure that these translations include all needed and adequate explicitations so that the reading may be both safe and useful and that Scripture can form the thinking of the faithful.

On the other hand, Scripture is meant not only for the Church's ministers or faithful but for all men. The Council recommends editions of the Bible with notes adapted to non-Christians.

Priests and people should try to distribute these editions discreetly. It is wholly in keeping with the spirit of Vatican II to show the universal character of all the spiritual goods of the Church and to desire that Scripture reach all men. It is also a sign that the Catholic Church thinks that the written Word of

God carries a message that can touch the hearts of men who do not believe. Thus the Council manifests the desire of the Catholic Church for total trust in, and submission to, the Word of God which is contained in Scripture and which brings the voice of the Holy Spirit wherever he wishes.

26. Epilogue

The Constitution closes with the plea that through the reading of Sacred Scripture, "the divine word be spread and glorified" (cf. 2 Thess. 3, 1), and the riches of revelation entrusted to the Church fill the hearts of all men. The Church has received nothing for herself. The Word of God that transmits and proclaims is free to accomplish its universal course and to fill the whole world along unforeseen paths. Certainly revelation is entrusted to the Church so that she may proclaim it to all men and initiate the great and universal dialogue of God with the whole human race. This deeply interior reality of the revelation of the Word of God written and transmitted concerns the whole universe. This beautiful Constitution on revelation closes on this universal note.

A final comparison between Scripture and the eucharist shows the unity of the Word and the sacrament alluded to at the beginning of Chapter VI. The life of the Church increases, thanks to the constant recourse of Christians to the eucharist. In the same way spiritual life grows in the Church, thanks to the increase of veneration for the Word of God. One of the triumphs of Vatican II will be to have increased the love of the Word of God in the Catholic Church: "a new impetus to her spiritual life may also be expected" and a new impetus to ecumenical life which can lead to the visible unity of all Christians, thanks to "a greater veneration of the Word of God 'which remains forever.' "

De Divina Revelatione

**THE
DOGMATIC CONSTITUTION
ON
DIVINE REVELATION
OF
VATICAN COUNCIL II**

**Promulgated by Pope Paul VI
November 18, 1965**

Some minor points should be noted concerning the following translation.

The references given in the text and all but one of the footnotes belong to the Constitution itself. The reader will notice that some of the biblical references specify that the Greek text of the New Testament is being quoted or alluded to. In all other instances, the reference is to the Latin Vulgate.

I have found it necessary to add a footnote of my own, the first in Chapter III. This is numbered 16a in order not to break the sequence of the Constitution's official footnotes. This footnote is self-explanatory.

All the official footnotes refer to biblical passages or ecclesiastical documents. In some cases they mention one or two recent editions where one may read the passage in question: I have put these between parentheses. References to Denzinger's *Enchiridion Symbolorum* contain two numbers: the first is that of the old edition, Denzinger-Bannwart; the second is that of the newer edition, Denzinger-Schönmetzer.

The few lines following the last chapter do not belong to the Constitution as such. They constitute the formula of promulgation. Although, for brevity's sake, Pope Paul's name alone follows, the Constitution was promulgated by the entire Council, that is, by Pope Paul together with the Council fathers.   GEORGE H. TAVARD

PAUL BISHOP

SERVANT OF THE SERVANTS OF GOD
TOGETHER WITH THE FATHERS OF THE SACRED COUNCIL
COMMITS TO PERMANENT RECORD

THE DOGMATIC CONSTITUTION
ON
DIVINE REVELATION

PROLOGUE

1. To the Word of God this holy Synod listens carefully. It proclaims it fearlessly and makes these words of St. John its own: "We announce to you the eternal life, which was with the Father and has appeared to us. We announce to you what we have seen and heard, that you may commune with us and that our communion be with the Father and with his Son, Jesus Christ" (1 John 1, 2-3). Following the Council of Trent and the first Council of the Vatican, it intends to explain the authentic doctrine concerning divine revelation and its transmission, so that the whole world, hearing, may trust the message of salvation—trusting, may hope—hoping, may love.[1]

[1] Cf. St. Augustine, *De catechizandis rudibus*, ch. IV, n. 8 (*P.L.*, p. 40, 316).

I
REVELATION

2. It has pleased God in his goodness and wisdom to reveal himself, and to make known the secret hidden in his will (cf. Eph. 1, 9): through Christ, the Word made flesh, and in the Holy Spirit, men have access to the Father and are made sharers in the divine nature (cf. Eph. 2, 18; 2 Pet. 1, 4). In this revelation the invisible God (cf. Col. 1, 15; I Tim. 1, 17), prompted by his overflowing love, addresses men as friends (cf. Ex. 33, 11; John 15, 14-15) and converses with them (cf. Bar. 3, 38) with the purpose of inviting and receiving them into communion with himself. This revelation is effected in interrelated actions and words: the works performed by God in the history of salvation point up and confirm the doctrine and the realities expressed by his words; the words proclaim his works and throw light on the mystery contained in them. Through this revelation the profound truth concerning God and human salvation shines for us in Christ, who is at the same time the mediator and the fullness of the whole revelation.[2]

3. God, who creates and preserves all through his Word (cf. John 1, 3), presents men with a perennial testimony to himself in created things. With the purpose of opening the way of salvation from heaven (cf. Rom. 1, 19-20), he furthermore manifested himself to our first parents in the beginning. After their fall, he raised them, by a promise of redemption, to hope in salvation (cf. Gen. 3, 15); and he watched over

[2] Cf. Matt. 11, 27; John 1, 14 and 17; 14, 6; 17, 1-3; 2 Cor. 3, 16 and 4, 6; Eph. 1, 3-14.

mankind without failing, ready to give eternal life to all those
who seek salvation by persistent well-doing (cf. Rom. 2, 6-7).
At his own good time he called Abraham to make him into a
great nation (cf. Gen. 12, 2); after the patriarchs, he taught
the nation, through Moses and the prophets, to acknowledge
him as the only living and true God, the prudent Father and
the just Judge, and to expect the promised Savior. Through
the centuries, he thus prepared the way for the Gospel.

4. After speaking many times in many ways in the prophets, God "finally, in these very days, has spoken to us in the
Son" (Heb. 1, 1-2). He sent his Son, the eternal Word who
enlightens all men, to dwell among men and tell them the se-
crets of God (cf. John 1, 1-18). Jesus Christ, therefore, the
Word made flesh, "a man sent to men",[3] "speaks God's
words" (John 3, 34) and fulfills the saving task entrusted to
him by the Father (cf. John 5, 36; 17, 4). To see him is to see
the Father (cf. John 14, 9). Thus, by all his presence and
self-manifestation, by his words and his works, by his symbolic
actions and his miracles, especially by his death and his glorious resurrection from the dead, he—the Spirit of truth being
finally sent—brings revelation to perfection by fulfilling it,
and confirms it with the divine witness: God is among us to
free us from the darkness of sin and death, and to raise us up
into eternal life.

The Christian order, which is the new and final covenant,
shall never pass away. No further public revelation is to be
expected until the glorious manifestation of our Lord Jesus
Christ (cf. 1 Tim. 6, 14; Tit. 2, 13).

5. To God who reveals himself is due the "obedience of
faith" (Rom. 16, 26; cf. Rom. 1, 5; 2 Cor. 10, 5-6), by which
man freely pledges himself to God, giving "God the full submission of his intelligence and will"[4] and voluntarily assent-
ing to the revelation he has made. For such a faith to be born,

[3] *Epistola ad Diognetum*, ch. VII, n. 4 (Funk: *Patres Apostolici*, I, p.
403).

[4] Vatican Council I, *Constitutio dogmatica de fide catholica*, ch. 3
(*Denz.* 1789; 3008).

man needs to be prepared and assisted by God's grace and the interior helps of the Holy Spirit, who will move and turn the heart to God, open the eyes of the mind and give "all men joy in consenting to and believing the truth".[5] Unceasingly, the same Holy Spirit so perfects faith through his gifts that the understanding of revelation may become more profound.

6. In divine revelation God has wanted to show and to share himself and the eternal decisions of his will concerning men's salvation, "that they may participate in the divine wealth, which utterly exceeds the human mind's comprehension".[6]

This holy Synod recognizes that "God, the beginning and the end of all things, may be known with certainty by the natural light of human reason reflecting on created things" (cf. Rom. 1, 20). It teaches, however, that it is due to revelation that "in the present condition of mankind, the divine realities, which are not in themselves beyond the reach of human reason, may be known by all in a short time, with firm certainty and without error".[7]

[5] 2nd Council of Orange, canon 7 (*Denz.* 180; 377); Vatican Council I, *loc. cit.* (*Denz.* 1791; 3010).
[6] Vatican Council I, *Constitutio dogmatica de fide catholica*, ch. 2 (*Denz.* 1786; 3005).
[7] *Ibid.* (*Denz.* 1785 and 1786; 3004 and 3005).

II

THE TRANSMISSION OF
DIVINE REVELATION

7. God mercifully provided that what he had revealed for the salvation of all nations should be integrally preserved forever and transmitted to all generations. For this purpose, Christ the Lord, in whom the entire revelation of God Most High is brought to completion (cf. 2 Cor. 1, 20; 3, 16-4, 6), commissioned the apostles to preach the Gospel to all—formerly promised through the prophets, and now fulfilled and orally proclaimed by himself—as the source of all saving truth and moral discipline: thus they would bestow God's gifts on men.[8] This was faithfully done by the apostles: in what they preached, did and instituted, they handed on what they had received from Christ, in his words, his way of life and his works, or what they had learned at the Holy Spirit's suggestions. This was also done by the apostles and the apostolic men who, inspired by the same Holy Spirit, wrote down the news of salvation.[9]

That the Gospel might be kept integral and alive without interruption in the Church, the apostles gave themselves successors, the bishops, to whom they handed on "their own teaching responsibility".[10] This holy transmission and the Holy Scripture of the two covenants are therefore like a looking glass in which the pilgrim Church on earth contemplates

[8] Cf. Matt. 28, 19-20; Mark 16, 15; Council of Trent, session IV, Decree *De Canonicis Scripturis* (*Denz.* 783; 1501).

[9] Cf. Council of Trent, *loc cit.*; Vatican Council I, session III, *Constitutio dogmatica de fide catholica*, ch. 2 (*Denz.* 1787; 3006).

[10] St. Irenaeus, *Adversus Haereses*, III, 3, 1 (*P.G.* 7, 848; Harvey, 2, p. 9).

God, from whom she receives all, until the time when she will be led to see him face to face as he is (cf. 1 John 3, 2).

8. Thus, the apostolic preaching, which is expressed in a unique way in the inspired books, had to be kept continually until the end of time. Whence, handing on what they themselves received, the apostles exhort the faithful to maintain the traditions they have learned, whether by word of mouth or by mail (cf. 2 Thess. 2, 15), and to fight for the faith once received (cf. Jude 3).[11] What has been transmitted by the apostles contains all that leads to the sanctification of the life of the People of God and to the growth of faith. Likewise the Church, in her doctrine, life and worship, perpetuates and transmits to all generations all that she is and all that she believes.

The Tradition that issues from the apostles progresses in the Church under the assistance of the Holy Spirit.[12] Insight into the realities and the words transmitted grows: this results from contemplation and study by the faithful who ponder over them in their heart (cf. Luke 2, 19 and 51), from their experience of a profound understanding of spiritual realities, from the preaching of those who, with the episcopal succession, received the unfailing charism of the truth. Through the centuries the Church always strives after the fullness of divine truth, until the ultimate fulfillment of God's words in herself.

The sayings of the holy Fathers witness to the life-giving presence of this Tradition, whose riches are poured into the experience and life of the believing and praying Church. Through the same Tradition, the integral list of the sacred books becomes known to the Church, and the sacred letters themselves are understood in their depths and made indefectibly contemporary in her. In this way, God, who spoke in the past, unceasingly talks to the bride of his beloved Son; and the Holy Spirit—through whom the living voice of the

---

[11] Cf. 2nd Council of Nicaea (*Denz.* 303; 602); 4th Council of Constantinople, session X, canon 1 (*Denz.* 336; 650-652).

[12] Cf. Vatican Council I, *Constitutio dogmatica de fide catholica*, ch. 4: *De fide et ratione* (*Denz.* 1800; 3020).

Gospel is raised in the Church and, through her, in the world —leads believers into all truth and makes the Word of Christ dwell in them abundantly (cf. Col. 3, 16).

9. Holy Tradition, then, and Holy Scripture are closely interconnected and they intercommunicate. For, flowing from the same divine source, they both somehow join into one and run toward the same end. Holy Scripture is God's own speech as written under the influx of the divine Spirit; by holy Tradition, God's Word, entrusted to the apostles by the Lord Christ and the Holy Spirit, is relayed integrally to their successors, so that, following the light of the Spirit of truth, these may faithfully preserve, expound and spread it in their discourses. Consequently, the Church does not draw her certainty about all that is revealed with the help of Holy Scripture alone. Both are, therefore, to be received and venerated with equal pious affection and reverence.[13]

10. Holy Tradition and Holy Scripture form the one sacred deposit of God's Word which has been entrusted to the Church. By adhering to it, all the holy People, together with its pastors, perseveres in the apostles' doctrine and communion, in the breaking of the bread and in prayer (cf. Acts 2, 42, Greek text). Thus, the remarkable harmony of bishops and faithful comes into being in the preservation, the practice and the confession of the traditional faith.[14]

The task of providing an authentic interpretation of God's Word in Scripture or Tradition[15] has been entrusted only to the Church's living magisterium,[16] whose authority is wielded in the name of Jesus Christ. This magisterium is not above God's Word; it rather serves the Word, teaching only what

[13] Cf. Council of Trent, session IV, *loc. cit.* (*Denz.* 783; 1501).

[14] Cf. Pius XII: Apostolic Constitution *Munificentissimus Deus,* Nov. 1, 1950 (*Acta Apostolicae Sedis* 42 [1950], p. 756) , with reference to the words of St. Cyprian, *Epistola 66,* 8 (Hartel, III, B, p. 733): "The Church, the people united to its Priest and the flock following its Shepherd . . ."

[15] Cf. Vatican Council I, *Constitutio de fide catholica,* ch. 3 (*Denz.,* 1792, 3011).

[16] Cf. Pius XII: Encyclical Letter *Humani generis,* Aug. 12, 1950 (*A.A.S.* 42 [1950], pp. 568-9; *Denz.* 2314; 3886).

has been transmitted, as, by divine mandate and with the Holy Spirit's assistance, it listens to God's Word with piety, keeps it in awe and expounds it with fidelity. All that it puts forward to be believed as divinely revealed, it draws from this one deposit of faith. Patently, therefore, Holy Tradition, Holy Scripture and the Church's magisterium are, according to God's wise design, so interconnected and united that none can stand without the others, and that all together effectively contribute, each in its own way, under the motion of the one Holy Spirit, to the salvation of souls.

III

HOLY SCRIPTURE: DIVINE INSPIRATION AND INTERPRETATION

11. Divine revelation, which is contained and presented in Holy Scripture, was committed to writing under the Holy Spirit's influx.[16a] Following the apostolic faith, our holy Mother the Church holds the complete books of the Old and the New Testaments, with all their parts, to be sacred and canonical. For, written under the Holy Spirit's inspiration (cf. John 20, 31; 2 Tim. 3, 16; 2 Pet. 1, 19-21; 3, 15-16), they are authored by God and have been handed on to the Church as such.[17] To compose the sacred books, God selected men whom

---

[16a] As published by the *Osservatore Romano* (Nov. 19, 1965), the Latin text of the Constitution contains this sentence in the following form: *"Divinitus revelata, quae in Sacra Scriptura litteris continentur et prostant, Spiritu Sancto afflante consignata sunt."* This was already the version voted on on October 19, 1965. However, the location of the word *litteris* here results from an editor's or a printer's error. This can be easily seen: whereas the above form of the sentence appears for the first time in the booklet presenting the amendments to the Council Fathers (*Schema Constitutionis Dogmaticae De Divina Revelatione: Modi a Patribus Conciliaribus propositi a Commissione Doctrinali examinati*, p. 40), the same booklet contains the sentence in another form on p. 32, where the meaning of the amendment is explained: *"Divinitus revelata, quae in Sacra Scriptura continentur et prostant, Spiritu Sancto afflante litteris consignata sunt."* The explanation given at this point, which makes sense in relation to *this* form of the sentence, cannot correspond to the form it has on p. 40. That *litteris* goes with *consignata* rather than with *continentur* seems also clear from a grammatical point of view. The previous schemas followed the pattern of p. 32, which therefore belongs to the text as endorsed by the Council in September 1965. It is this version which our translation follows.

[17] Cf. Vatican Council I, *Constitutio dogmatica de fide catholica*, ch. 2 (*Denz.* 1787; 3006); Biblical Commission, Decree of June 18, 1915 (*Denz.* 2180; 3629; *Enchiridion Biblicum*, 420); Holy Office, Letter of Dec. 22, 1963 (*E.B.* 499).

he assisted in the use of their faculties and talents;[18] since he acted in and through them,[19] they, as genuine authors, would write all that he wanted and no more.[20]

Since all that the inspired authors or sacred writers assert must be considered as asserted by the Holy Spirit, one should affirm that the books of Scripture teach firmly, faithfully and without error the truth that God decided to put down in the sacred writings for our salvation's sake.[21] Thus, "every Scripture is divinely inspired and useful: it educates, it argues, it corrects, it teaches discipline, that the man of God may be perfect and instructed in every good deed" (2 Tim. 3, 16-17, Greek text).

12. In Holy Scripture God spoke through men in a human way.[22] In order to discern what he wanted to communicate to us, the interpreter of Holy Scripture must carefully seek what the sacred writers truly meant and God gracefully revealed in their words.

Among other things, the "literary forms" are to be considered in order to find out the sacred writers' purpose. Truth is diversely presented and expressed in texts that are, in varying degrees, historical, prophetical, poetical, or belong to other forms of speech. Moreover, the interpreter ought to inquire into the meaning which, in his precise circumstances, the sacred writer intended to, and did, express, given the conditions of his time and culture and the nature of the literary forms

---

[18] Cf. Pius XII, Encyclical Letter *Divino afflante Spiritu,* Sept. 30, 1943 (*A.A.S.* 35 [1943], p. 314; *E.B.* 556).

[19] On *"in* and *through* man",* cf. Heb. 1, 1 and 4; 4, 7 (*in*); 2 Sam. 23, 2; Matt. 1, 22 and *passim* (*per*); Vatican Council I, *Schema de doctrina catholica,* note 9 (Coll. Lac., VII, 522).

[20] Leo XIII, Encyclical Letter *Providentissimus Deus,* Nov. 18, 1893 (*Denz.* 1952; 3293; *E.B.* 125).

[21] Cf. St. Augustine: *Gen. ad litt.* 2, 9, 20 (*P.L.* 34, 270-1); *Epistola 82, 3* (*P.L.* 33, 277; *CSEL* 34, 2, p. 354); St. Thomas, *De veritae,* q. 12, a. 2, C; Council of Trent, session IV, *De canonicis scripturis* (*Denz.* 783; 1501); Leo XIII, Encyclical Letter *Providentissimus Deus* (*E.B.* 121, 124, 126-7); Pius XII, Encyclical Letter *Divino afflante Spiritu* (*E.B.* 539).

[22] St. Augustine: *De civitate Dei,* XVII, 6, 2 (*P.L.* 41, 537; *CSEL* XL, 2, 228).

then in use.[23] For, in order to understand what the sacred author wanted to say in writing, one has to take due account of the customary, indigenous ways of feeling, of speaking or of telling a tale, which obtained in the sacred author's times, and of those commonly used in human relations in that period.[24]

Scripture must be read and interpreted in the same Spirit in whom it was written.[25] To find out correctly the sense of the sacred texts, one must therefore consider with no less care the content and the unity of Scripture as a whole, paying attention to the living Tradition of the whole Church and to the analogy of faith. Exegetes are to work along those lines toward a deeper understanding and explanation of the meaning of Holy Scripture; and, thanks to this scholarly preparation, the Church's discernment will mature. For all these points concerning scriptural interpretation are ultimately subject to the Church's discernment: she fulfills the divine mandate and task of watching over and interpreting the Word of God.[26]

13. The wondrous descent of the eternal wisdom to our level is thus evident in Holy Scripture, while the truth and holiness of God are respected. "Thus we may learn the unutterable kindness of God, and how he adapted his speech, in his providence and care for our nature." [27] For the words of God, expressed in human tongues, became similar to human language, just as formerly the Word of the eternal Father, assuming flesh with its human weakness, became similar to man.

[23] St. Augustine: *De doctrina Christiana*, III, 18, 26 (*P.L.* 34, 75-6).

[24] Pius XII, *loc cit.* (*Denz.* 2294; 3829-3830; *E.B.* 557-62).

[25] Cf. Benedict XV, Encyclical Letter *Spiritus Paraclitus*, Sept. 15, 1920 (*E.B.* 469); St. Jerome: *In Galat.* 5, 19-21 (*P.I.* 26, 417A).

[26] Cf. Vatican Council I *Constitutio dogmatica de fide catholica*, ch. 2 (*Denz.* 1788; 3007).

[27] St. John Chrysostom, *In Genesim*, 3, 8 (hom. 17, 1) (*P.G.* 53, 134). *Attemperatio* [tr. as: "adapted his speech"] corresponds to the Greek word *synkatábasis*.

IV
THE OLD COVENANT

14. God, who in his love carefully planned and prepared the salvation of all mankind, chose for himself, by a unique decision, a People whom he would entrust with his promises. By a covenant with Abraham (cf. Gen. 15, 18) and, through Moses, with the People of Israel (cf. Ex. 24, 8), he revealed himself, in words and deeds, as the only true and living God to the People he had acquired. Thus, Israel was destined to discover by experience which were God's ways with men, to understand them more deeply and clearly day by day when God spoke through the prophets, and to spread their knowledge among the nations (cf. Ps. 21, 28-29; 95, 1-3; Is. 2, 1-4; Jer. 3, 17). The design of salvation, foretold, detailed and explained by the sacred authors, stands out, as God's true Word, in the books of the Old Covenant. For this reason these divinely inspired books keep their permanent value: "Whatever was written, was written for our instruction, that, through perseverance and with the help of the Scriptures, we may have hope" (Rom. 15, 4).

15. The order of the old covenant was structured, above all, so as to prepare the advent of Christ, the universal redeemer, and his messianic kingdom, to announce him in prophecy (cf. Luke 24, 44; John 5, 39; 1 Pet. 1, 10), and to show him through various images (cf. 1 Cor. 10, 11). In ways adapted to the state of mankind before the time when Christ initiated salvation, the books of the Old Covenant reveal to all the knowledge of God and of man and the ways in which the just and merciful God deals with men. Although they also contain imperfect

and provisional elements, these books nevertheless describe the true divine pedagogy.[28] They are to be received with devotion by the Christian faithful. For they express a true awareness of God. Splendid teachings about him, a healthy wisdom on matters of human life and admirable treasures of prayers are also stored up in them. Finally, the mystery of our salvation is enfolded in them.

16. God, the inspirer and author of the books of both Covenants, wisely caused the New to be latent in the Old, and the Old patent in the New.[29] Christ established the new covenant in his blood (cf. Luke 22, 20; 1 Cor. 11, 25); nonetheless, the books of the Old Covenant, assumed in their totality in the preaching of the Gospel,[30] acquire and manifest their full meaning in the new covenant (cf. Matt. 5, 17; Luke 24, 27; Rom. 16, 25-26; 2 Cor. 3, 14-16), which they in turn illustrate and explain.

[28] Pius XI, Encyclical Letter *Mit brennender Sorge,* March 14, 1937 (*A.A.S.* 29 [1937], p. 151).

[29] St. Augustine: *Quaestiones in Heptateuch* 2, 73 (*P.L.* 34, 623).

[30] St. Irenaeus: *Adversus Haereses,* III, 21, 3 (*P.G.* 7, 950); (=25, 1: Harvey 2, p. 115); St. Cyril of Jerusalem, *Catecheses* 4, 35 (*P.G.* 33, 497); Theodore of Mopsuestia, *In Soph.* 1, 4-6 (*P.G.* 66, 452D-453A).

V
THE NEW COVENANT

17. The Word of God is God's saving power for all believers (cf. Rom. 1, 16). It is manifest and efficacious most of all in the books of the New Covenant. For, when the fullness of time had come (cf. Gal. 4, 4), the Word was made flesh and dwelt among us, full of grace and of truth (cf. John 1, 14). Christ inaugurated the kingdom of God on earth; by his actions and his words he showed his Father and himself; he completed his work in his death, his resurrection and his glorious ascension and in the sending of the Holy Spirit. Being raised above the earth, he who alone has the words of eternal life (cf. John 6, 68) draws all men to himself (cf. John 12, 32, Greek text). This mystery was not unveiled to other generations as it has now been revealed in the Spirit (cf. Eph. 3, 4-6, Greek text) to the holy apostles and prophets so that these might preach the Gospel, awake faith in Jesus, the Christ and Lord, and gather the Church together. The writings of the New Covenant subsist as a permanent and divine record of these facts.

18. Everybody knows that the Gospels rightly stand out among all the Scriptures, even those of the New Covenant. For they are the main record of the life and teaching of the Word incarnate, our Savior.

Always and everywhere the Church has taught, as she does now, the apostolic origin of the four Gospels. What the apostles preached on Christ's order, they and some apostolic men, under the Holy Spirit's influx, later transmitted to us in writing: this is the foundation of the faith, the fourfold Gospel according to Matthew, Mark, Luke and John.[31]

19. Our holy Mother the Church has firmly and constantly taught, as she does now, that these four Gospels, whose historicity she affirms without hesitancy, faithfully report what Jesus, the Son of God, in the course of his life among men actually did and taught until the day of his ascension for their eternal salvation (cf. Acts 1, 1-2). Indeed, after the Lord's ascension, the apostles reported to their audiences the things which he had said and done, with the fuller insight which they enjoyed,[32] once they had learned from Christ's glorious destiny and they were enlightened by the Spirit of truth.[33] Sacred authors wrote the four Gospels; some things they sorted out from among many that were transmitted orally or already in writing; some they brought together into a synthesis or they interpreted in keeping with the state of the Churches; in brief, they preserved the style of proclamation in order always to share with us true and authentic records of Jesus.[34] Whether from their own memory and remembrance or on the witness of those who "saw him from the beginning and were ministers of the Word", they wrote with the purpose that we might know the "truth" of the words which we have been taught (cf. Luke 1, 2-4).

20. Besides the four Gospels, the canon of the New Covenant also contains the letters of St. Paul and other apostolic writings composed under the Holy Spirit's inspiration. According to God's wise design, these confirm what relates to Christ the Lord; they make his genuine teaching better and better known; they announce the saving power of the divine work of Christ; they tell the story of the beginnings and the

[31] Cf. St. Irenaeus: *Adversus Haereses*, III, 11, 8 (*P.G.* 7, 885; Sagnard, ed., p. 194).

[32] John 2, 22; 12, 16; cf. 14, 26; 16, 12-13; 7, 39.

[33] Cf. John 14, 26; 16, 13.

[34] Cf. Biblical Commission, Instruction *Sancta Mater Ecclesia* (*A.A.S.* 56 [1964], p. 715).

admirable spread of the Church; and they foretell her glorious consummation.

For, as he had promised (cf. Matt. 28, 20), Christ was present with his apostles, and he sent them the Paraclete, the Spirit, to lead them into the fullness of truth (cf. John 16, 13).

VI
HOLY SCRIPTURE
IN THE CHURCH'S LIFE

21. The Church has always venerated the divine Scriptures like the Lord's body itself. Especially in the sacred liturgy, she never stops taking the bread of life from the table which is both that of the Word of God and that of the body of Christ, and offering it to the faithful. She has always considered them, as she does now, together with Holy Tradition, as the supreme rule of her faith. For having been inspired by God and set to writing once for all, they unfailingly communicate the Word of God himself, and they embody the voice of the Holy Spirit in the words of the prophets and apostles. Like the Christian religion itself, all Church proclamation must feed on, and be ruled by, Holy Scripture. In the sacred books, the Father who is in heaven lovingly approaches his children and talks to them. The Word of God contains such force and efficacy that it stands out for the Church as nourishment and health and, for the Church's children, as strength of their faith, food for their soul, pure and perennial font of their spiritual life. These sayings apply excellently to Holy Scripture: "The Word of God is alive and active" (Heb. 4, 12); "it has the power of building up and sharing the heritage among all the saints" (Acts 20, 32; cf. 1 Thess. 2, 13).

22. Access to Holy Scripture must be wide open to the Christian faithful. For this purpose the Church at the beginning already received as her own the old Greek translation known as the *Septuagint*. The Church also always honors the other Oriental translations and the Latin translations, and

first of all the one called the *Vulgate*. Since God's Word must be available at all times, the Church's maternal care sees to it that opportune and correct translations, especially from the original texts of the sacred books, are printed. If, at the appropriate occasion and with the approval of the Church's authority, they are prepared jointly with separated brethren, all Christians will be able to use them.

23. The bride of the incarnate Word, the Church taught by the Holy Spirit, endeavors to reach a deeper understanding of the Holy Scriptures in order always to feed her children with divine utterances. She therefore duly fosters the study of the holy Fathers of both East and West and of sacred liturgies. Catholic exegetes and the other students of sacred theology should zealously unite their efforts and, under the vigilance of the sacred magisterium, work at the investigation of the sacred letters with appropriate means. Their aim should be that as many ministers of the divine Word as possible may fruitfully provide the People of God with the nourishment of the Scriptures: it will enlighten the minds, strengthen the wills and attract the hearts of men to the love of God.[35] This sacred Synod encourages the Church's children who labor in the biblical field, that, renewing their strength every day, they may steadfastly pursue, according to the mind of the Church, the completion of the work happily begun.[36]

24. As upon a permanent foundation, sacred theology rests upon the written Word of God in unity with holy Tradition. In this Word it finds strong support and ever new youth as it examines in the light of faith all the truth hidden in the mystery of Christ. The Holy Scriptures contain the Word of God and, on account of their inspiration, they are the Word of God. Accordingly, the study of the sacred text should be, so

---

[35] Cf. Pius XII, Encyclical Letter *Divino afflante Spiritu* (*E.B.* 551, 553, 567); Biblical Commission, *Instructio de S. Scriptura in Clericorum Seminariis et Religiosorum Collegiis recte docenda*, March 13, 1950 (*A.A.S.* 42 [1950], pp. 495-505).

[36] Cf. Pius XII, *ibid.* (*E.B.* 569).

to speak, the soul of sacred theology.[37] The ministry of the Word also—namely, pastoral preaching, catechetical teaching and all Christian instruction, in which the liturgical homily should occupy a privileged place—is fed healthily and thrives in holiness, thanks to the same Word of Scripture.

25. It is therefore necessary for all clerics, and first of all for priests and for those who are lawfully engaged in the ministry of the Word as deacons and catechists, to devote themselves to assiduous sacred reading and careful study of the Scriptures. Otherwise, someone who must dole out to the faithful in his care the abundant wealth of the divine Word, especially in the sacred liturgy, might become "exteriorly a vain preacher of God's Word, not being interiorly a hearer of it".[38] This holy Synod also insistently and particularly exhorts all the Christian faithful and, above all, the religious, to learn "the eminent knowledge of Jesus Christ" (Phil. 3, 8) through frequent reading of the divine Scriptures. "For to ignore the Scriptures is to ignore Christ." [39] Let them therefore willingly approach the sacred text itself, through the sacred liturgy, which is filled with the divine Words, through pious reading, and through the appropriate organs and other helps which are fortunately multiplied everywhere in our days with the encouragement and assistance of the Church's pastors. Let them remember, however, that prayer should accompany Scripture reading for a conversation to take place between God and man; for "we speak with him when we pray, and we hear him when we read the divine maxims".[40]

It belongs to the bishops, "among whom the apostolic doctrine resides",[41] to prepare the faithful in their care, at the

[37] Cf. Leo XIII, Encyclical Letter *Providentissimus Deus* (E.B. 114); Benedict XV, Encyclical Letter *Spiritus Paraclitus* (E.B. 483).

[38] St. Augustine: *Sermon* 179, 1 (P.L. 38, 966).

[39] St. Jerome: *Comment. in Isaiam*, Prol. (P.L. 24, 17); cf. Benedict XV: Encyclical Letter *Spiritus Paraclitus* (E.B. 475-80); Pius XII: Encyclical Letter *Divino afflante Spiritu* (E.B. 544).

[40] St. Ambrose: *De officiis ministrorum*, I, 20, 88 (P.L. 16, 50).

[41] St. Irenaeus: *Adversus Haereses*, IV, 32, 1 (P.G. 7, 1071); (=49, 2 Harvey 2, p. 255).

right time, to make proper use of the divine books, especially of those of the New Covenant and first of all the Gospels. This should be done through translations of the sacred texts, to which necessary explanations that should be truly sufficient are attached. Thus the Church's children will safely and fruitfully converse with the Scriptures and be steeped in their spirit.

Furthermore, let editions of Holy Scripture, with appropriate notes, be published also for the use of non-Christians to whose conditions they should be adapted. Both those who have pastoral functions and Christians of whatever state should take care to distribute them wisely in any way possible.

26. Through reading and studying the sacred books, "the divine Word is spread and clarified" (cf. 2 Thess. 3, 1), and the treasury of revelation entrusted to the Church fills the hearts of men more and more. As the Church's life increases through continuous access to the eucharistic mystery, a new impetus to her spiritual life may also be expected from a greater veneration of the Word of God, which "remains forever" (Is. 40, 8; cf. 1 Pet. 1, 23-25).

*   *   *

Each and every point stated in this Constitution has satisfied the fathers of the sacred council. And we, by the authority bestowed on us by Christ, together with the venerable Fathers, approve it in the Holy Spirit, we decree it and we enact it; and we order the promulgation, to God's glory, of what has been enacted synodically.

Rome, in St. Peter's Basilica, November 18, 1965

Paul, Bishop of the Catholic Church
(The Fathers' signatures follow)

SELECTED BIBLIOGRAPHY

Chapter I:
  Balthasar. Hans Urs von. *Word and Revelation*. New York:
    Herder & Herder, 1964.
  Bulst, Werner. *Revelation*. New York: Sheed & Ward, 1965.
  Rahner, Karl, and others. *The Word: Readings in Theology*.
    New York: P. J. Kenedy & Sons, 1964.
  Semmelroth, Otto. *The Preaching Word*. New York: Herder
    & Herder, 1965.

Chapter II:
  Moran, Gabriel. *Scripture and Tradition: A Survey of the
    Controversy*. New York: Herder & Herder, 1963.
  Tavard, George. *Holy Writ or Holy Church*. New York:
    Harper, 1959.
  Vawter, Bruce. *The Bible in the Church*. New York: Sheed
    & Ward, 1959.

Chapter III:
  Daniel-Rops, Henri. *What Is the Bible?* New York: Haw-
    thorn Books, Inc., 1958.
  Levie, Jean. *The Bible, Word of God in Words of Men*.
    New York: P. J. Kenedy & Sons, 1958.
  Schökel, Luis A. *The Inspired Word*. New York: Herder &
    Herder, 1965.
  Steinmann, Jean. *Biblical Criticism*. New York: Hawthorn
    Books, Inc., 1958.

Chapter IV:
  Flanagan, Neal. *Salvation History*. New York: Sheed &
    Ward, 1964.

McKenzie, John L. *The Two-Edged Sword.* Milwaukee, Wis.: Bruce Publishing Co., 1956.

McKenzie, R. A. F. *Faith and History in the Old Testament.* University of Minnesota, 1963.

Chapter V:

Auzou, Georges. *The Word of God.* St. Louis, Mo.: B. Herder Book Co., 1960.

Bouyer, Louis. *The Meaning of Sacred Scripture.* University of Notre Dame, 1958.

Schnackenburg, Rudolf. *New Testament Theology Today.* New York: Herder & Herder, 1963.

Chapter VI:

Charlier, Celestin. *The Christian Approach to the Bible.* Westminster, Md.: Newman Press, 1958.

Daniélou, Jean. *The Bible and the Liturgy.* University of Notre Dame, 1956.

Swidler, Leonard, ed. *Scripture and Ecumenism.* Duquesne University Press, 1965.

Tavard, George. *Theology of the Word.* New York: Paulist Press, 1963.

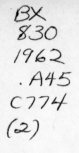